D1133556

MOULDING
AND
GLASS FIBRE
TECHNIQUES

Other titles in this series include:

Installing Radio Control Equipment   Peter Smoothy
Setting up Radio Control Helicopters   Dave Day
Building from Plans   David Boddington
Basic Radio Control Flying   David Boddington
Flying Scale Gliders   Chas Gardiner
Operating Radio Control Engines   Brian Winch and David Boddington
Covering Model Aircraft   Ian Peacock

Moulding and Glass Fibre Techniques

Peter Holland

ARGUS BOOKS

Argus Books
Wolsey House
Wolsey Road
Hemel Hempstead
Hertfordshire HP2 4SS

First published by Argus Books 1989

ISBN 0 85242 981 9

Phototypesetting by GCS, Leighton Buzzard
Printed and bound in Great Britain by
William Clowes Ltd, Beccles

Contents

Chapter 1
Introduction

IF YOU BUILD models from published plans or your own designs, it may well be that you can use a commercial canopy, cowling or other ready-moulded component, even if it has to be modified in some way. But what if the plan specifies other than an available moulded part, or your design needs something special in that respect?

This book is intended to show how mouldings can be made at home easily and at low cost, exactly to suit your own particular model. It covers the various types of materials, from heat-formed plastic sheet through laminates such as GRP to casting rubber in moulds, as well as applications, including strengthening structures and achieving superior finishes. It suggests forms of construction, shows how others can be modified or repaired and helps kit purchasers to join, fit and finish those ready-made components.

A nicely moulded cockpit canopy always sets a model off well.

Fig. 1. Key—1. Foam veneered fuselage halves. 2. Foam veneered wings. 3. Foam veneered fin. 4. Foam veneered turtle deck. 5. Moulded plastic canopy. 6. Plastic cockpit interior. 7. Air intake halves. 8. Jet pipe. 9. Wing tip tank balsa cores. 10. Wing tip tank plastic outer halves. 11. Pre-assembled tank/engine bay. 12. Balsa sheet tailplane. 13. Self-adhesive roundels/stickers. 14. Lexan sheet. 15. Information sheets. 16. Instruction booklet.

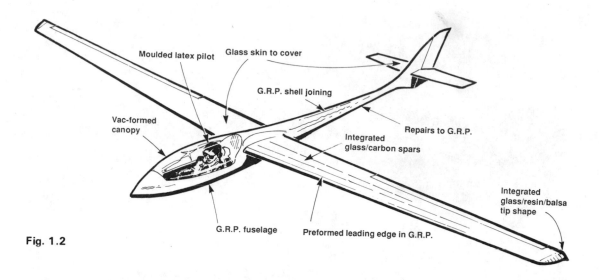

Fig. 1.2

Where?

A basic glider employing a number of moulded features is shown in Fig. 1.2 but a power model's finishing touches could also include a hard-wearing cowling round the engine, undercarriage fairings, small fairings at control-rod exits and further moulded components as shown applied to a scale subject in Fig. 1.3. Add in the major components employing glass fibre and the blend of materials and mouldings can be seen; indeed, you are probably using those materials already. Now find out how to create special components to make your model strong, give it an air of realism and, if it is to be a scale subject, make those scale details durable and repeatable.

The book deals with the subject material by material rather than detail by detail; as this maintains the theme of 'while your hands are sticky... as it were.

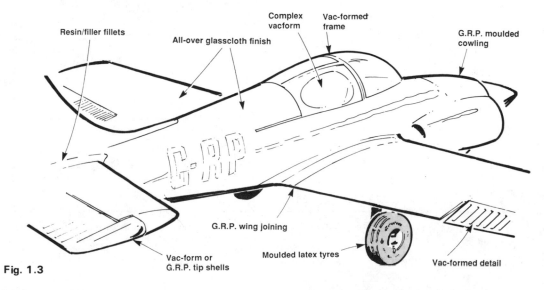

Fig. 1.3

Chapter 2
Heat forming sheet materials

THE FIRST ITEM that springs to mind when considering heat moulding is the cockpit canopy. Purchased ready-made it should be smooth and clear, not like some we have seen produced by the modeller in a great hurry, probably by the wrong method for the job. These may be rather bumpy and covered with an interesting but unnecessary wood grain effect which renders them partially opaque.

It is this very item that lowers the quality of an otherwise well finished model aeroplane. Let a few tips make that canopy better and see how the same forming methods can yield many useful items for the model.

The materials

Several sheet plastic materials are suitable for use by the modeller. Which ones are used, and their attributes may be seen from Table 1. The thickness of the sheet will be related to the size and depth of the moulding to be made. Fig. 2.1 shows what happens when plastic sheet, softened by the application of heat, is stretched to follow a shape. Clearly a deep shape will make the sheet so thin that an already thin piece of material will break into a hole. An unnecessarily thick sheet in a shallow shape is heavy and wasteful, and if the shape is intended to have

Table 1

MATERIAL	FUEL RESISTANCE	CLARITY	MOULDABILITY	STRENGTH	RISK OF BLUSHING	COST
ABS	Good	Good	Good	Good	Nil	Moderate
ACETATE	Poor	Fair	Good	Fairly good	Yes, if too cool	Low
BUTYRATE	Fair	Very good	Quite good	Fair	Nil	Moderate
LEXAN	Good	Very good	Good	Exceptional	Nil	High
PERSPEX	Good	Good	Good	Fair	Nil	Fairly high
STYRENE	Good	Good	Good	Fair	Nil	Low
VINYL	Good	Very good	Good	Good	Nil	Moderate

IMPORTANT: Some plastic sheet - material is also available in non-mouldable grade, ie., Acetate, Perspex, etc., so make sure you specify   "Moulding Grade".

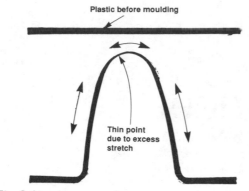

Plastic before moulding

Thin point
due to excess
stretch

Fig. 2.1

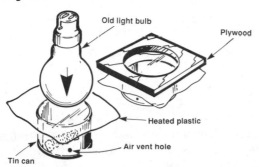

Old light bulb

Plywood

Heated plastic

Air vent hole

Tin can

Minimum surface
detail

Epoxy filled surface

Clearance angle

Mounting spigot
or handle

Extra depth

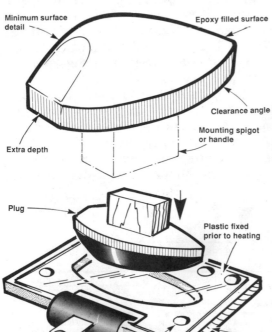

Plug

Plastic fixed
prior to heating

Plywood plate
to fit plug
plus plastic
thickness x 2

Clips or drawing pins

Fig. 2.2

sharp corners: these will be rounded.

The reason for this latter is that it is usual to make the component by stretching the sheet over a forming block known as a 'plug' and it is generally easier to make a solid plug rather than create a hollow. Furthermore, the plastic has its own smooth surface to view, ironing out tiny imperfections that would otherwise be transferred from the surface of the plug.

The technique

There are two methods of heat forming sheet: The simplest, but limited in application, is the Pressure method. Here a plug in the shape of the intended component is fitted with a handle and forced by hand into a sheet of plastic which has been fixed to a plywood frame and heated until it is flexible. The plywood has a hole cut in it, to force the plastic to follow closely to the sides of the plug. Fig. 2.2.

While this method does work for simple shapes, it is no match for vacuum forming, where the plug is mounted on the perforated lid of a box, and the plastic is fixed to a frame that can be rapidly and accurately dropped in place over the plug. Air is then sucked out of the box and from around the plug. Atmospheric pressure then presses the plastic firmly down all round. See Fig. 2.3 for the principle.

In both methods, the plastic retains the shape of the plug on cooling and, provided the plug has clearance, can be lifted off and the edges trimmed away close to the required shape.

The crafts room of most schools may well have a purpose-made moulding machine, and if one has connections in that direction, all that needs to be done is to provide a plug and the sheet of material.

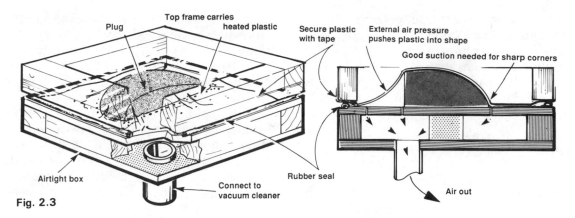

Fig. 2.3

Labels in Fig. 2.3:
Plug
Top frame carries heated plastic
Secure plastic with tape
External air pressure pushes plastic into shape
Good suction needed for sharp corners
Airtight box
Rubber seal
Connect to vacuum cleaner
Air out

Plugs

Block balsa might seem to be a quick and easily worked material for the plug, but on its own it is not ideal. It is soft and even if the surface has been sanded smooth and filled, it may be crushed by the pressure of thick plastic. Really hard balsa, jelutong or a softwood such as pine will in the long run offer a surface that can receive a hard, smooth finish, essential if that 'wood-grain' effect is to be avoided.

Plan the shape, remembering that it has to be removed from the finished moulding. If there is a bulge on the sides of, say, a canopy, the bottom edges may be smaller than mid way up the side, a sure way to frustration. Such shapes have to be made in sections, as seen in Fig. 2.4. If the position of canopy frames precludes this, then the plug itself needs to be made in sections, a tricky business, as the joints in the plug have to be made to coincide with dummy frame lines (Fig. 2.5). At this point it should be decided whether to make a plug to include ridges to represent frames or merely to indicate the position of frames to be applied after fitting to the model. Unless the plastic is very thin and vacuum forming of a high 'pressure' is used, the frame ridges are likely to be less crisply defined, particularly where

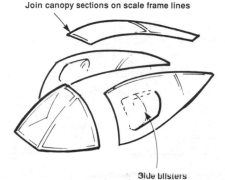

Join canopy sections on scale frame lines

Side blisters

Fig. 2.4

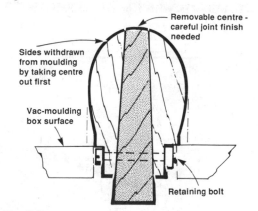

Removable centre - careful joint finish needed
Sides withdrawn from moulding by taking centre out first
Vac-moulding box surface
Retaining bolt

Fig. 2.5

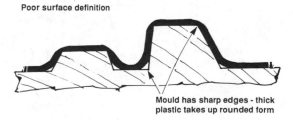

Poor surface definition

Mould has sharp edges - thick plastic takes up rounded form

Fig. 2.6

the 'frame' meets the 'glazing'. This is because the plastic cannot be forced around sharp internal corners by atmospheric pressure when the suction is supplied, for example; by a domestic vacuum cleaner. Fig. 2.6.

A simple vac-forming unit

Compared with the plugs, this item is relatively easy to make. The perforated top is perforated hardboard, which, although flexible, can be supported underneath. Alternatively, ³⁄₁₆ or ¼in. (4–6mm) ply is better for larger sizes. The holes are still needed, with similar spacing but advantageously smaller, at

¹⁄₁₆ in. The author's unit is framed with 1in. square softwood and has a disused plastic lid screwed underneath to sit over the end cap of a cylinder type vacuum cleaner, which is stood on end for the occasion. The frame which is to hold the sheet of plastic is more 1in. square timber and there are locating strips of light alloy angle at the rear corners, angled slightly out to avoid fumbling when transferring the frame and hot plastic from the domestic oven to the vac-unit.

A strip of silicone rubber fuel or waterjacket tube is epoxied or applied with contact adhesive around the smooth, un-perforated edge of the box to make an airtight seal with the plastic

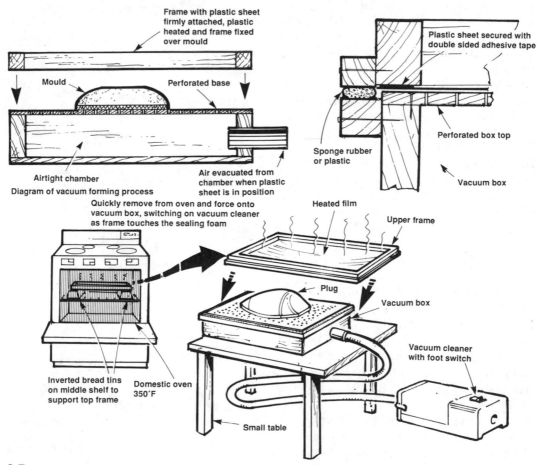

Frame with plastic sheet firmly attached, plastic heated and frame fixed over mould

Mould

Perforated base

Airtight chamber

Diagram of vacuum forming process

Air evacuated from chamber when plastic sheet is in position

Plastic sheet secured with double sided adhesive tape

Sponge rubber or plastic

Perforated box top

Vacuum box

Quickly remove from oven and force onto vacuum box, switching on vacuum cleaner as frame touches the sealing foam

Heated film

Upper frame

Plug

Vacuum box

Inverted bread tins on middle shelf to support top frame

Domestic oven 350°F

Vacuum cleaner with foot switch

Small table

Fig. 2.7

on its frame. Fig. 2.7 shows the general arrangement.

Heating the plastic

First ascertain that you have selected the right type of plastic sheet for the job. Some look alike, but behave differently. Clear sheet, for example, may be ABS, which is fine for the job, but there are moulding grades of acetate sheet and grades intended for using flat. The latter do not stretch when heated. Perspex acrylic sheet comes in rigid and moulding grades; difficult to tell apart. Do not use 'acrylic sheet' intended for glazing at D.I.Y. shops—it is not intended for moulding. It will stretch and can be heat bent, but after a few days becomes brittle and crazes where stress has been imposed on it. It also reacts unfavourably to some paints and even some polishes. Clearly a material for home glazing only. Softer polyvinyl sheet also stretches, but is not capable of retaining the intended shape accurately. The thrifty will cut up clear plastic fizzy drink bottles and if the shape they yield does not fit the job, re-heat and give them a second lease of life. It's a matter of experiment here, but if the correct material is bought and labelled for future use, there should be no confusion or disappointment.

A small sample of the material may be heated under the domestic grill or in the oven. When it appears to be floppy, grasp it with two pairs of pliers and stretch it. It should pull into a thin strip before parting. If it does not, then it is the wrong type of plastic or it is not quite hot enough. Swift action at the right time is what is needed. Overheating will cause blisters to form, roughening the surface and making it partly opaque. Delaying the moulding will allow the sheet to cool and resist stretching.

Some modellers detect the point when the sheet is ready to mould by watching for first a slight sag, then a slight recovery, then a second sag. Others time the heating needed for a sample of given thickness. This and the oven temperature tend to be subject to experiment. Ovens vary, and so does the speed of the operator.

Ideally, the heat source should be on the moulding machine, but for simplicity a practised technique of removing the hot sheet on its frame from the oven at the right time and promptly placing it over the plug then switching on the vacuum cleaner (in less time than it takes to read this) brings success.

Larger mouldings

The domestic oven will not heat the larger sheets of plastic needed for mouldings of, say, 14in. and longer. Furthermore, the handling and rapid transfer of the frame to the moulding unit is not always possible with accuracy. Overcoming these problems is the purpose of the combined unit in Fig. 2.8. It has the advantage that the plastic is heated evenly right up to the time that moulding takes place. As the frame carrying it is positioned directly over the vacuum unit, pulling it away from close proximity to the heating unit to enclose the plug is almost instantaneous. There is the advantage that there is still some radiant heat available to slow the cooling process down, thus giving the vacuum time to operate effectively.

With the oven heating method, this continued heat application can only be obtained by pointing a heat gun or similar source at the area around the plug, after the vacuum is turned on. Not having three hands, this is likely to result in burnt holes in the thinly

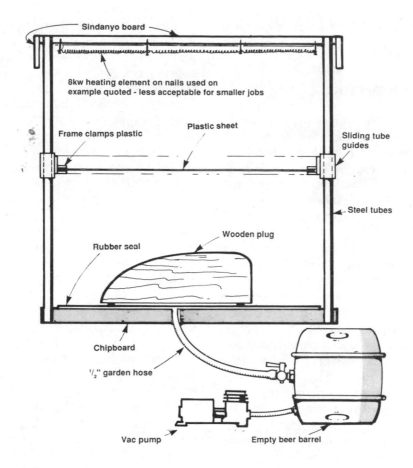

Sindanyo board

8kw heating element on nails used on
example quoted - less acceptable for smaller jobs

Frame clamps plastic

Plastic sheet

Sliding tube
guides

Steel tubes

Wooden plug

Rubber seal

Chipboard

¹/₂" garden hose

Vac pump

Empty beer barrel

Fig. 2.8

stretched plastic!

Caution should be exercised in making the heater for the combined unit, however, for mains voltage is being employed. The mountings for the element should be insulated to prevent shorts and the wiring leading to the ends of the element should be of high temperature specification. All connections and wiring must be properly insulated—seek the

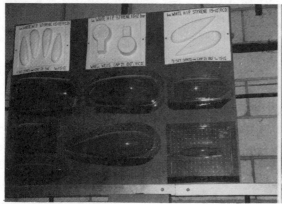

Commercial mouldings in different grades of white and clear plastic.

A plug in position in a commercial vacuum-forming machine.

help of a proper electrician to check that the unit is safe.

One point about vac-forming is that when shallow forms are attempted there is not much stretch, so a false move is retrievable; the plastic can be re-heated if it did not form correctly, provided that it was not pierced or separated from the frame.

There is no difference in vac-forming opaque sheet, for use as fairings, cowling parts, blisters, wing-tips and housing pods. Corrugated panels may be made for scale subjects, those ribbed skin reinforcement panels on control surfaces, for example. Small components can be grouped on the moulding box for production at one 'go'. If a single item is small, the plastic sheet may be secured with masking tape to a rectangle of thin card or thick paper, to bring it up to frame size (Fig. 2.9). Allow space around the subject, however, to provide some plastic from which to stretch, otherwise the edge will pull away from the tape and the plastic will be wasted.

Finishing off

Having released the plastic from the frame, gently ease the plug from the moulding. Do not press the moulding down to free the plug; ease the edge to admit air. If necessary insert a screw into the plug if it is not already fixed to the box by a keyhole slot. Wiggle it lightly until it loosens fully. With scissors or metal shears, trim away all but ½–¼in. of waste from around the moulding, (Fig. 2.10) which should also have a slight upstand around its intended base. This will keep it rigid enough for handling and any final polishing. Commercial mouldings have large areas of plastic around them, so that they retain their shape in storage—they are quicker to produce that way too.

A commercial vac-forming machine.

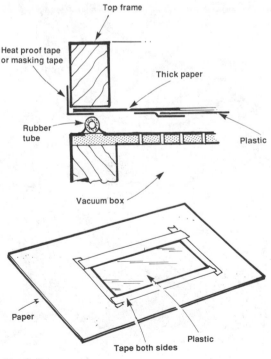

Top frame

Heat proof tape or masking tape

Thick paper

Rubber tube

Plastic

Vacuum box

Paper

Plastic

Tape both sides

Fig. 2.9

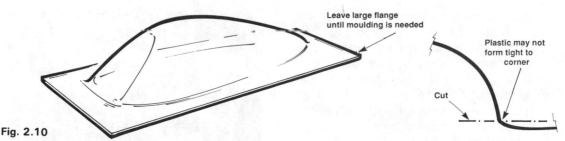

Leave large flange
until moulding is needed

Plastic may not
form tight to
corner

Cut

Fig. 2.10

Do not try to trim off large areas close to the moulding—it may distort it or the scissors or knife may score the surface or even crack it.

Fitting and trimming

If anything looks untidy, it is a mis-aligned cockpit canopy, but some fuse-lage contours will try to defeat your efforts in getting the thing to sit square. A tip worth remembering is to make a dummy canopy on a piece of paper taped over the model, as seen in Fig. 2.11.

The junction of the Plasticine and the paper is where the glazing edge should be. Without distorting the Plasticine, transfer it into the canopy moulding, where it should fit snugly. Holding it still, draw around the joint line with a chinagraph pencil on the outside of the canopy. Cut on the waste side of this line to allow an overlap if the canopy has to overlap the cockpit edge, or on the line if it has to fit flush inside. Trim it down in stages, to make sure that the dummy has not moved or distorted.

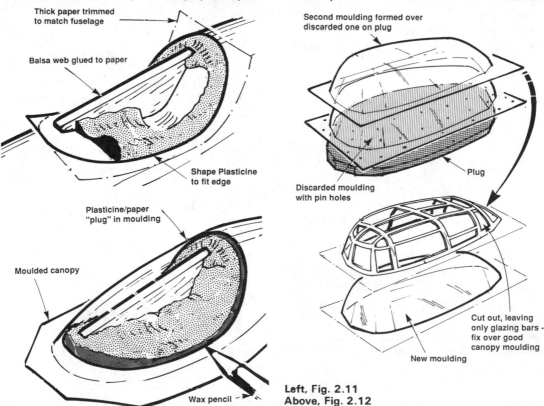

Thick paper trimmed
to match fuselage

Balsa web glued to paper

Shape Plasticine
to fit edge

Plasticine/paper
"plug" in moulding

Moulded canopy

Wax pencil

Second moulding formed over
discarded one on plug

Plug

Discarded moulding
with pin holes

Cut out, leaving
only glazing bars -
fix over good
canopy moulding

New moulding

Left, Fig. 2.11
Above, Fig. 2.12

Remember that once the canopy is in place, chances of painting cockpit detail or the inside face of any canopy frames have gone!

A touch or two of cyano adhesive will hold the canopy in position while it is epoxied finally to the fuselage. First, though, apply a thin strip of masking tape around the edge, leaving only the area that will later be painted free for glueing. This will prevent smudges of epoxy on the clear areas. Apply the epoxy sparingly so that it does not run inside, wipe clear any excess and strip the masking tape away before it has fully cured. An alternative to epoxy, at least for British modellers, is 'Modellers' Glue', an adhesive sold under that name.

Separate frames

If a second moulding is made from the original plug, then pierced and replaced on the plug, a third moulding can be taken over this combined plug. It will be larger than the first full moulding and can be cut away to leave only complex framework lines. This skeleton then fits over the finished moulding after it has been painted. The result can be neater

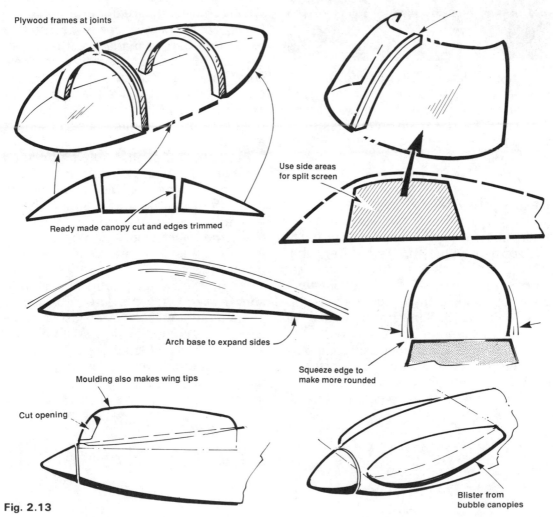

Plywood frames at joints

Ready made canopy cut and edges trimmed

Arch base to expand sides

Moulding also makes wing tips

Cut opening

Use side areas for split screen

Squeeze edge to make more rounded

Blister from bubble canopies

Fig. 2.13

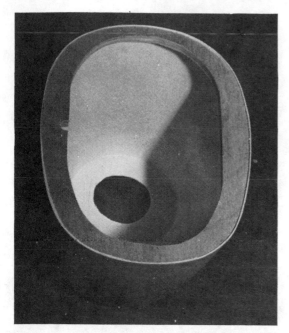

A plug for moulding a cowling. For vacuum-forming it would be necessary to blank off the front hole. With a cowling this deep a two-part forming would be preferable.

than the application of separate strips of thin ply, plastic sheet or metal representing the glazing frames and bars. See Fig. 2.12. One for the scale enthusiast, this, but mentioned here because it involves vac-forming.

Patch and match

That next model may have need for a vac-formed shape that is not from the last moulding. Rather than modify the plug or make another, consider adjusting an existing moulding—some ideas appear in Fig. 2.13. The same tricks can be tried with commercial mouldings: the fertile mind will suggest using canopy mouldings for wing-tips or parts of them for blisters and cowling parts—who will know the difference when painted?

Planning a shape

When designing a plug for a cowling, for example, remember that there is a limit to the amount of stretch, or 'draw' as it should be known. Mould only the front ring of radials, make separate blisters on, say a Jungmeister cowl, and form only the front panel of apple cheek jobs, which makes the rear parts easier to form. There is no reason to include areas that can be made from flat sheet or those that have single curvature. Yes, commercial mouldings are deep, tough, and may well be in one piece, but they are formed on industrial machines and the home moulder has to be a little less ambitious.

Remember that although the finished component may have a hole in it, a large one in the case of radial cowls, the moulding must be made 'blind'—holes will not work in vac forming. Trim it out later, the spare plastic can be used for detailing, just like any other piece of plastic sheet.

Practise on small items, using thin sheet, then once the knack of vac or press moulding is acquired larger items can be attempted with less chance of wastage. It is a clean process, but wear thick gardening gloves or, if you can work in them, oven mitts—it is surprisingly hot!

Chapter 3
Basic glass fibre laminating

ONE OF THE most widely used techniques for reinforcement of model airframes, right through to the production of complete fuselages, even complete wings, is that of glass reinforced plastics, or GRP for short.

Strands of spun glass are the structural members; the strongest form is a woven cloth which is also lighter than chopped strands formed into a 'mat'—the type of material supplied in most motor repair kits, together with epoxy or polyester resin and matching hardener, which is a catalyst. The purpose of the resin mixture is to bond the strands of glass together and to the adjacent structure. The resultant material is resilient and very strong, but heavier than the balsa and ply it may be used to replace. Very thin GRP can be formed by specialised processes. This can be stronger than traditional construction for no extra weight penalty, permitting slimmer, high efficiency wings to be made for, as an example, the more competitive soarer.

Epoxy resins are stronger and lighter than polyester types. They are less brittle and combined with glass cloth result in a more efficient form of lamination or reinforcement.

Wing joining

In order to become acclimatised to working with the material, the joining of a pair of wing halves is a typical exercise. Many kits supply foam-cored veneered wing panels and while in many cases the instructions offer very specific advice for glass-fibre reinforcement of the centre joint, a few presume some knowledge of the procedure on the part of the modeller. Let's do it right first time—GRP is irreversible and once it has hardened (or 'cured' as it is more properly termed) it cannot be softened, melted or torn apart without wrecking the adjacent structure.

If foam wings are being joined, the very first thing to do is to ensure that polyester resin, the more commonly sold bonding agent, (e.g. car repair kits) DOES NOT come into contact with the foam core. It eats away at the core under the veneer, undetected, then when the joint is stressed, the centre folds up.

For this reason the bonding agent should be epoxy resin and its appropriate hardener. '5 minute' epoxy can be used—but unless one works fast, the one or 3 hour types are better. Epoxy resin, unlike the polyester types, does

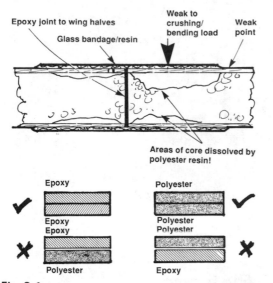

Fig. 3.1

It may not be appreciated, that epoxy and polyester resins do not bond effectively to each other. For this reason, it is false economy and unnecessarily messy to apply epoxy resin to, for example, the veneer over the area to be covered in bandage and polyester resin. Fig. 3.1 should serve as a reminder.

not affect expanded polystyrene and is equally or often more effective in bonding the glass cloth or glass bandage that is to reinforce the joint. It costs a little more than polyester resin and its accompanying hardener, but even after making a good job of butt-joining the wing cores with epoxy, there is a chance that some small gap or crack in the veneer will admit even the vapour of polyester resin, should this be used in the re-inforcement stage.

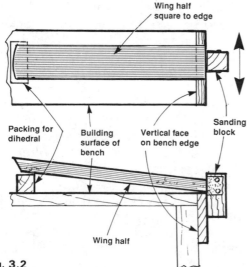

Fig. 3.2

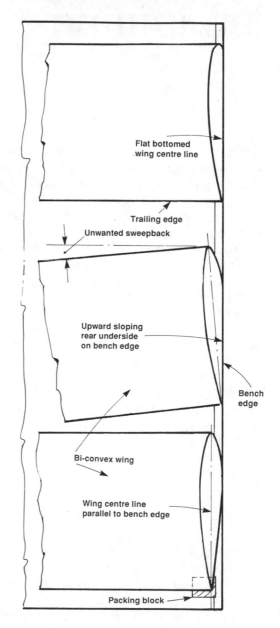

Fig. 3.3

20

Alignment

If the wings have one straight edge or are of parallel chord, the alignment of each half prior to joining is made easier. Fig. 3.2 suggests a simple jigging arrangement to aid accuracy. If the end of the building board has a deep face to it, this can guide a wide sanding block when trimming the root faces of the wing panels, once the tip ends are propped up for dihedral, if specified, or weighted down flat if there is to be none. Bi-convex wings need packing at the trailing edge so that they adopt an attitude that brings the datum line level. If this is not done, the wings will have unwanted sweep-back—Fig. 3.3 explains why.

Check that you finish up with a left and a right wing half, each with the top surface on top. This may sound elementary, but suppose a veneered foam wing has parallel chord and a section that is not symmetrical, but not obviously flat bottomed. Haste driven by enthusiasm can result in two right or two left wings, or one lifting normally and one 'lifting' downwards. Fig. 3.4 advises identification.

When both root faces are sanded so that they meet fully, masking tape can be used to hinge the flatter edges below. Apply the epoxy to core and veneer edges, hinge back together and place on polythene over a flat board with the trailing edges sharing the same piece of packing under the polythene. Pack the tips if there is dihedral and lean a weight against each tip to apply endwise pressure to the joint. Make a final inspection to check alignment which will be verified if a finger nail can slide smoothly from side to side over the joint at the leading edge and trailing edge and near those points on the top surface. When the epoxy has just passed the 'rubbery' stage of cure, before it is fully

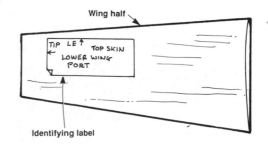

Fig. 3.4

hardened, trim away any blobs of epoxy that may have been squeezed out. They will make the joint reinforcement lumpy otherwise, perhaps misaligning the wing on its seat, if they are near the leading or trailing edge.

Reinforcement

To be effective, the centre reinforcement should spread out gradually to avoid a sudden change in strength, for such results in a weak point and can cause a wing to fail at the edge of the bandage. Ideally a central strip of bandage, say 2in. wide, is covered by a layer of thin glass cloth about 4in. wide. This blends the strength into the veneer gradually. Fig. 3.5. Both layers go right round leading and trailing edges and under the wing. Arrange the joint under a high wing or over a low wing, to be out of sight. If there is to be an aileron servo mounting hole, bandage right over and cut it clear while the epoxy is set but not hard. On models where the wing is fairly thick, the bandage can be stopped short of the servo position.

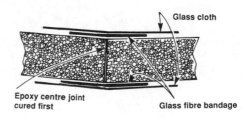

Fig. 3.5

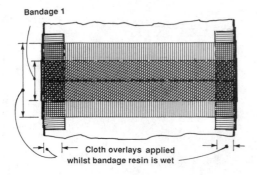

Bandage 1

Cloth overlays applied
whilst bandage resin is wet

Fig. 3.6

Those wings which have veneer right over the leading edge and brought together at the trailing edge will benefit from strips of glass tape extending out past the position of wing retaining rubber bands, or an inch past the fuselage edge where bolt-on fixing is used. Fig. 3.6. The strongest job results when all the subsequent layers of cloth or bandage are applied while this initial layer is wet.

Cutting the cloth

The strands of glass will fray easily when cut and the bits get everywhere; brush them aside and you will get itching fingertips. Never blow them away, since they might get breathed in or get in the eyes.

For accuracy and safety, run a light line of dope along the intended cutting line. When dry, this seals the edge and prevents the slippery strands from skewing out of square. Masking tape also restricts fraying during cutting—tape outside the cut line, Fig. 3.7. Lay the cut pieces down in order so that the right one is to hand as needed. Once wetted with resin it will be sure to fold up into a tangle when lifted off, should the wrong piece be used, particularly if it is lightweight grade.

Caution. Before handling any resins or hardeners, apply an appropriate barrier cream to the hands—GRP suppliers recommend and should supply one that is best for the job. Wear polythene gloves as an alternative or additional protection. These can be purchased at chemists.

Some people's skins are very sensitive to the resin, so be prepared. Odd splashes should be washed off immediatly should they escape the protected area. Cellulose thinners followed by hot soapy water is advised.

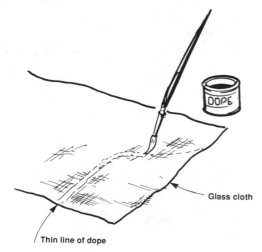

DOPE

Glass cloth

Thin line of dope

Fig. 3.7

Mixing

Small packs of resin and hardener usually come with mixing instructions and some provide a suitable mixing measurement cup. Those which are of thick consistency have to be squeezed out in a strip so that appropriate proportions can be mixed. The runnier types are ideal for applying cloth to skin wings and for lightweight laminating jobs. Mix these by weight in a disposable plastic or paper cup, for if any mixed resin is left in the container it may reduce the quality of subsequent mixes. Furthermore the added weight spoils the calculations.

Place the container on light duty kitchen scales—those designed for low weight full scale deflection are more accurate for this purpose. Zero the pointer to account for the weight of the cup. Pour in resin and note the weight. For a 50/50 mix add hardener until the weight doubles. For other proportions, calculate the total weight by adding the percentage—easy on the grams scale. Always add hardener to resin, not the other way round.

Bonding

A wing of 8in. chord should take less than 4 minutes to coat with mixed epoxy and work into the bandage. Hot weather shortens the working time available, so if it is decided to use a '5 minute' epoxy, avoid mixing more than can be properly worked in before it becomes rubbery.

It is better to apply the epoxy thinly, more easily done if a thin, runny resin is purchased. More only adds weight. If air bubbles can be seen in the weave, press the tape down and if they are still there, add a little more epoxy and stipple it down with a stiff brush. Expect to see the texture of the weave, for a smooth surface indicates excess. The strongest mixture is when the layers of glass are close together with the minimum of epoxy between. Remember to get the following glass layer applied while the first resin is 'wet'.

Apply masking tape to the wing to mark the edge of the reinforcement and prevent the epoxy spreading out too far. Lay and epoxy the wider glass cloth, smoothing out any bubbles. Do not aim for a fully filled smooth surface at this stage; it is more important to get the cloth to bond. If when this is done, the surface is still really wet, dust some talcum powder over it to aid smoothing later. Sellotape at the edge feathers it off (Fig. 3.8).

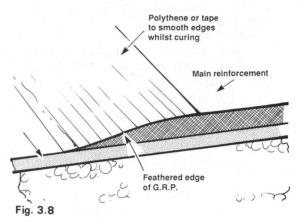

Fig. 3.8

Cleaning up

After all the reinforcement is fully cured, lightly sand the surface with wet and dry abrasive paper on a large block. Do not go further than to take off roughness. Avoid cutting into the glass strands and go very gently towards the masking tape, so that the veneer is untouched. Take the tape off and tackle the edge with fine grade paper working up onto the glassfibre, but never down into the veneer. The section in Fig. 3.9 shows what happens with heavy sanding. Remember that it is the veneer that provides the strength, not the core.

Balsa wings

Traditional built-up balsa wings can be

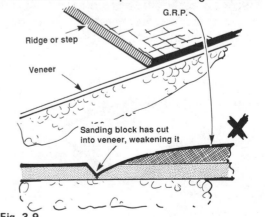

Fig. 3.9

joined by exactly the same method, except that if high strength/weight is not so important polyester resin mix can be used in place of epoxy resin. The working time may be longer, depending on the amount of catalyst or hardener necessary. In all cases, follow the makers' instructions—different brands have different mixes, one hardener may not work with another resin. Mixing containers and old brushes can be cleaned with cellulose thinners before the resin has fully cured.

Tips

Whereas some 5 minute epoxy is fairly thick and can be mixed in small quantities on a flat surface, other forms of epoxy, intended for skinning applications, are thinner and need to be mixed in the bottom of a plastic cup. Five-minute epoxy can be mixed up on a few strips of masking tape on a scrap of board, the tape discarded afterwards. In hot weather, lay the tape on a thick tile or piece of smooth house brick and leave it in the freezer for a while before mixing the epoxy on the tape. This will lengthen the working life of the mix which remains on the tape. (Fig. 3.10).

In the early stages of working the resin into the bandage, the application of gentle heat from a hair drier will make it spread easily, but prolonged use will speed the cure. Remember that curing cannot be halted or reversed.

Fig. 3.10

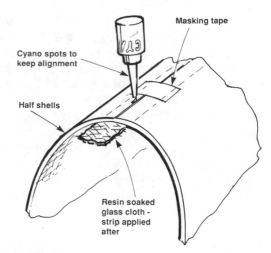

Fig. 3.11

Joining GRP components

Some kits provide GRP fuselage half shells, or fins that have to be joined to the fuselage. A neat and secure joint is usually required on the INSIDE. At first sight, this may seem difficult. Few fuselages are large enough to get one's hand and a brushful of resin inside. Added to this, there is the problem of positioning and rubbing down the strip of bandage that strengthens the joint. See Fig. 3.11.

First, and most importantly, check with the instructions or specification to see if the shells are polyester bonded, if so, then polyester resin must be used in joining them—epoxy resin is not compatible. The most usual method of applying the bandage is seen in Fig. 3.12. Make up a rod from thick wire—coat hanger wire will do for small models. It has to be long enough to reach the tail end after inserting it at the wing position. The end is bent at 90 degrees and fitted with a piece of drilled ¼in. dowel wide enough to accept the tape. Slide a couple of short slices of fuel tubing onto the wire each side of the dowel, to retain it, but allow it to turn freely.

Use masking tape to hold the shell halves together and rub some wax polish over the outside where the joint shows. This will prevent any stray drips of resin marring the finish, should they escape through the joint. Do not apply wax under the masking tape; it will prevent it from sticking where it should. Rub the tape down well to prevent resin creeping under it. Only when satisfied that everything is aligned, prepare the joining tape. Cut a piece each for top and bottom joins. Lay out the bottom strip and coat it with resin mix. Pick up one end and hold it to the roller, making sure that loose strands are clear of the 'axle'. Roll it along, helping the tape to pile evenly and tightly onto the roller, by turning the roller with a piece of wire or a nail as shown in Fig. 3.13. Transfer the roller and tape to the inside of the joint and allow the loose end of the tape to lie flat along the joint. Hold it there with a scrap of wood or clip it to a convenient projection with a clothes peg. Steadily push the wire down inside the fuselage, keeping it right over the joint and moving it slightly to and fro to ensure

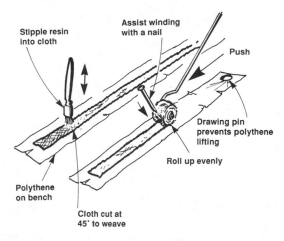

Fig. 3.13

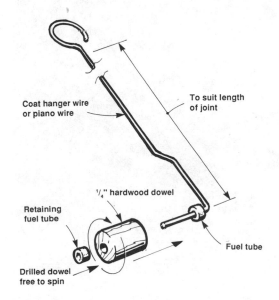

Fig. 3.12

contact and avoid the tape lifting When the roller reaches the tail end, wedge the rod so that it is undisturbed until the resin is firm but not cured past a 'cuttable' stage. Fish down inside and pull the remains of the tape clear of the roller if it has not already detached itself. Snip off any excess.

Clean the roller, clearing the hole if necessary, and repeat the procedure for the upper joint, this time with the fuselage propped up inverted at 45 degrees, so that the tape lies against the joint. A clothes peg will hold the front end of the tape against the wing seat.

Fin halves can be joined by the same method on a similar scale, or a piece of tape laid against a strip of wood which has been wrapped in cling film, so that it will release afterwards. The fin to fuselage joint is usually a simple overlap, so resin alone does the job—Fig. 3.14.

Outside, pick off the blobs of resin and sand the joint with fine wet and dry abrasive paper, used wet. Any further filling is done at the painting stage with the appropriate surfacing mix—polyester for standard polyester shells. The sanding should have removed any remaining release agent on the shells, ensuring a bond.

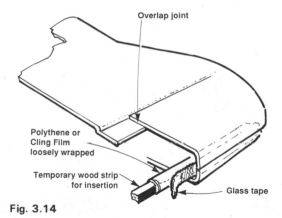

Fig. 3.14

Labels on Fig. 3.14:
- Overlap joint
- Polythene or Cling Film loosely wrapped
- Temporary wood strip for insertion
- Glass tape

Once again remember that epoxy is not compatible with polyester, so ply bulkheads, engine bearers etc. should be attached to polyester type fuselages with polyester resin. Similarly, where polyester resin is used to bond glass-fibre reinforcement into the nose area of a model of balsa construction, the same type of resin should be used to secure bearers, fixing blocks and to fuel-proof the area. If it is intended to fit these items with epoxy, then the reinforcement should be done with epoxy too.

A two-part GRP cowling. The monocoupe characteristics of GRP mean that internal structure can be dispensed with, making access much easier.

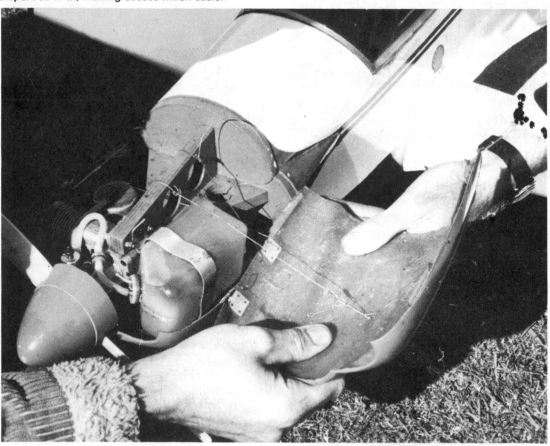

Chapter 4
Mouldings

THE MAKING OF shapes in glass-fibre can be done in two ways: laminating, which is a continuation of the method described for wing joint reinforcement, and cast moulding, where a mixture of resin and chopped strands is poured into a mould. For our purposes, the latter is unnecessarily heavy and the mould-making complicated. Most GRP components for radio controlled model aircraft are made by the lay-up method now to be described.

While it is possible to produce cowlings etc., by a method similar to that of wing joint reinforcement, the smoothing of the outside would probably take longer than it would take to make a mould for the purpose. Nevertheless, this method will be described later, for it is strictly a 'one-off' job.

We are concerned in producing a moulding which has exactly the right shape outside, not only made smooth where it needs to be but reproducing surface detail such as panel lines and rivet heads. All this in a durable material and repeatable should a second model be built.

At the same time, the moulding can be made thicker and stronger where stress points occur; in a fuselage this might be at the nose, wing fixing points, stiffening ribs inside, and thinned out at the tail end. Dual curvature not only adds rigidity to the moulding, but is no more difficult to produce than a straight taper.

Basically, the method, seen in Fig. 4.1, goes like this. A 'plug' is made to the shape of the outside of the intended moulding. If an existing model has the right shaped fuselage or cowling, it may be possible to use it as a plug, otherwise it can be built up with expanded polystyrene, covered in paper or planked with balsa, or made over formers in the traditional balsa modelling technique. It does not have to be strong, for it will be supported when it is used, but the finish must be blemish free. Over this plug a female mould is formed, either by casting in plaster of paris, or, more durably, in glass fibre itself. A release agent (PVA) which coats the surface of the plug permits the latter to be withdrawn, so after cleaning, the inside face of the female mould will be ready to transfer its shape to a finished moulding. Details for making the GRP mould follow later.

On goes a coat of release agent, this time in the mould. When this is dry, a thin mixture is made of polyester resin, to which has been added filler powder, colouring and lastly hardener (the catalyst). This is to be outside finish of the

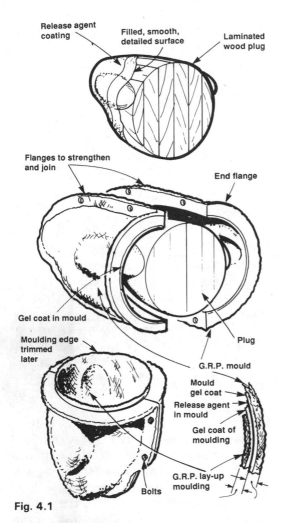

Release agent coating

Filled, smooth, detailed surface

Laminated wood plug

Flanges to strengthen and join

End flange

Gel coat in mould

Plug

Moulding edge trimmed later

G.R.P. mould

Mould gel coat

Release agent in mould

Gel coat of moulding

G.R.P. lay-up moulding

Bolts

Fig. 4.1

moulding and is known as a 'Gel coat'. (Remember that hardener is in proportion to the resin, not the mix of resin, filler and colouring. Some packs, though, have integrated filler, so follow the instructions accompanying the materials you have purchased). Before this coat is set hard, but not so runny that it can be disturbed, a mixture of resin and hardener is applied. This is followed immediately by glass fibre chopped strand mat or glass cloth. Subsequent layers are built up and the moulding left to cure. It can then be eased out of the mould and after trimming the edges, joined to other mouldings or the rest of the model. Now let us deal with each stage in detail, for each depends on the quality of the preceding one. A blemish becomes transferred or magnified. A part which does not fit can be traced right back to the original plug, so that is where to start.

Plugs

A cowling is a good starting point. Suppose it is deep and has apple cheeks. It has been decided to make it as a one-piece moulding, so that there are no outside joints. Later it will be cut for access to the engine. The shape has been designed like the one in Fig. 4.2.

The first consideration is that of clearance. Will the finished moulding come out of the mould? Indeed, will the mould come off the plug? Check from the drawing to see if the mould will have clearance. Fig. 4.3 shows what to look for. It might be supposed that the glass fibre moulding, being rather flexible, could be worked out of the mould. How, though, is the plug to come out first?

There are answers to this one, but these apply more to smaller items and a different method to be described much later. Then, back to the drawing board . . .

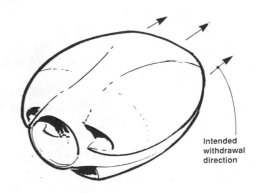

Intended withdrawal direction

Fig. 4.2

Is a slightly different shape acceptable? Perhaps the model is a scale subject. Does the whole of the cowling have to be moulded in one piece, can it be done with a separate front or divided down the centre, as might have been done with a vac-formed version? (Fig. 4.4).

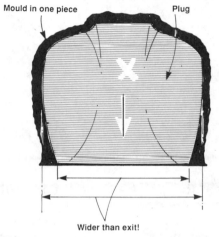

Fig. 4.3

Consider then, masking the plug off in sections, so that it can be set up to form several sections of mould. The mould parts will come off easily, and when they are clamped or bolted together, the finished moulding *can* be in one piece. Unclamping the mould sections will free it. This avoids any joining of the moulding

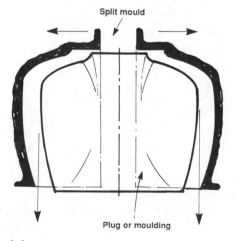

Fig. 4.4

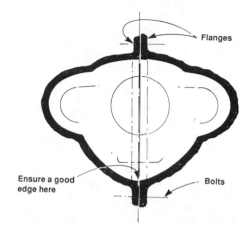

Fig. 4.5

itself. Fig. 4.5. shows how the plug is used to form mould sections.

There are, however, some points to remember: Surface detail on areas where there is little clearance in the mould for withdrawing the plug has to be minimal, otherwise it will effectively lock the plug into the mould being

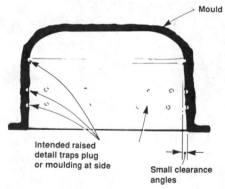

Fig. 4.6

made—see Fig. 4.6. The joints in the mould will probably show on the finished one-piece moulding. They will appear as ridges. These can be smoothed down after, but any raised detail near them will be smoothed off in the process. Similarly, panel line surface detail which crosses a joint will be interrupted and very careful alignment of the mould sections will have to be made to avoid that line becoming a 'joggle', see Fig. 4.7.

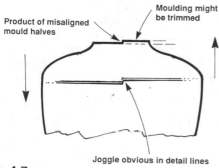

Fig. 4.7

Split plugs

Continuing the theme of a cowling, the correct alignment of two halves of a two piece moulding can be assured by the following method of making a plug.

Suppose a plug is to be made for producing a vac-form that has to be in two halves, say, split on the vertical centre line. Although the plug is made to

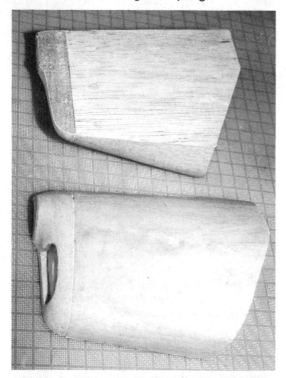

A split plug for moulding a cowling requires temporary depth increase on the separation line on each half.

be carved as one, for the sake of symmetry, it can be divided for use as separate halves. How this is done will facilitate the alignment later.

A series of laminations of hard balsa can be arranged each side of the centre line, but the adjacent centre laminations are prepared as shown in Fig. 4.8.

It will be remembered that vac-forms need to be deeper than the plug proper,

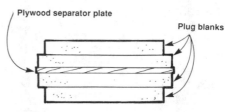

Fig. 4.8

so that the web between the moulding and the waste does not rob the moulding of any width. To carve the plug with this in mind might hamper the shaping, because there would be no definite transition between the plug shape and the allowance for the 'upstand' between it and the moulding table.

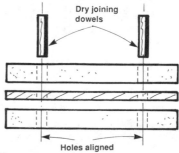

Fig. 4.9

It will be realised that the two halves of the moulding are taken from halves of the plug, each with this upstand. At this point, the choice is open for a glassfibre version to be made from the same plug. This is fine, provided one does not mind the latter being smaller, by the thickness of the moulding sheet. There are thus two alternative methods of dividing the plug for this purpose—first, as in

Fig. 4.9, for vac forming, assemble sheet balsa or pine from which the two centre laminations are to be cut to sandwich a spacer lamination of ply, the latter to be the thickness of the upstand on one half. Drill through all three pieces and insert wood dowels to locate them. Saw the resultant sandwich to the shape of the centre profile, plus a

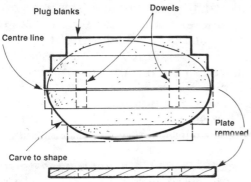

Fig. 4.10

sanding allowance. Next, remove the ply lamination and replace the centre laminations on the dowels and with the centre joints left dry, glue extra laminations each side to build up the plug to the correct width, as in Fig. 4.10. Carve and sand to finish, then fill and polish.

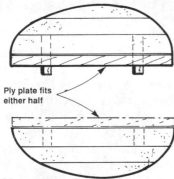

Fig. 4.11

The plug then separates, but can accommodate the ply spacer on one, or other half (Fig. 4.11). It will locate correctly on either and when moulded, each half shell should match when trimmed to the top of the spacer line.

The making of a glass fibre mould, split for the removal of the moulding,

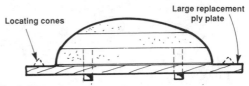

Fig. 4.12

can be done as follows—first substitute a wider ply centre lamination, sealed and finished with holes drilled in it, their positions being determined by the use of the ply spacer lamination made for the vac-form version. Either plug half should now fit with the pegs onto this ply plate. (Fig. 4.12). Coat the plug half and ply with release agent and proceed as described a little further on.

Drill bolt holes through the ply plate into the mould flange just produced, before removing the plug. Remove the plate and use the dowels to locate the

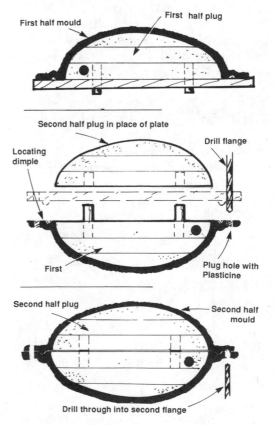

Fig. 4.13

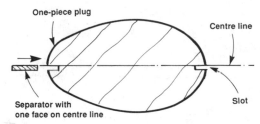

Fig. 4.14

other plug half, without the plate between. The meeting face of this half should be waxed to prevent the release agent glueing it to the plate! Fill the bolt holes with wax or Plasticine, apply release agent to the flange and plug. Continue as before then drill through the plugged holes into the new flange. The sequence is seen in Fig. 4.13.

When the mould halves are separated, they should align accurately and the bolt holes should match up. It is the bolts rather than locating cones or blisters that do this, so use bolts that are a perfect fit in the holes. Cones can also be incorporated in the first flange as seen in 4.13.

Dividing a one-piece plug

A purpose-made plug can be made with a well-marked line down the centre, that is to say a line which will guide a

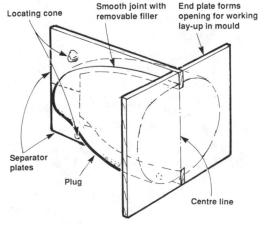

Fig. 4.15

sawcut which has one edge exactly on the centre of the plug. Sounds complicated, but look at Fig. 4.14. Suppose the plug is solid or laminated balsa, filled with sealer and sanded until it is smooth and blemish-free, since any wood grain effect will be transferred to the finished product (like the vac form referred to earlier in the book). Detail is added by scribing, fixing paper overlays, indenting with the end of a brass tube for screw heads, using pin heads or spots of PVA glue for rivets, etc., all this sealed and secured to ensure that the mould does not displace it in the process of being applied to the plug.

That sawcut will go through a detail here and there if they are placed close to the centre line. Into the sawcut, which should be about ¼in. deep, goes a piece of thin plywood or sheet aluminium, which will divide one part of the mould from its adjacent one. One face of the ply or metal will be on the centre line.

The ply has to be in two pieces, so that it can be fitted and removed. Insert it in the slots and seal the edge facing the centre line with a smear of soft filler, which can be removable; a scraping of soap or Plasticine will serve. This is to make a clean sharp edge to the mould and to prevent resin creeping into the sawcut and locking the parts together. The plug should now look like Fig. 4.15. Note the two little conical lumps of wood or Plasticine, which are later to form locating dimples in the mould flange when it is made, and the end plate which is fixed to the plug and will later form an open end, through which the moulding can be made.

A glass fibre mould

Support the plug and its ply divider in a horizontal position with the treated surface uppermost. Coat the entire top surface with release agent, not forgetting the ply. When this is dry, cut some glass fibre mat into strips large enough to cover the plug and a margin ½in. or so wide around it to form a flange. Cloth can be used, but is more expensive and weight saving is unnecessary here.

Mix up a gel coat, including the filler which will aid any final polishing. Only sufficient gel coat should be applied to fill detail and cover the rest of the plug like a coat of paint. One purpose of a gel coat is to avoid the weave or texture of the glass cloth or mat showing on the surface as a series of bumps and hollows. If there were tiny bubbles, these might form pits.

Apply the gel coat with a paint-brush or pad of sponge plastic on a stick (one tends to forget to clean the fast setting mixture off in time, so these can be expendable). Avoid forming bubbles in the coat as the mixture is worked into corners. Wipe out any deep puddles that form. It is possible to include a proportion of 'thixatropic' additive in the resin. This makes it hold onto vertical areas. Too much of this makes the gel coat thicker and difficult to brush out.

Check that the pieces of mat are ready to hand in the right pattern—lay them out in the same shape as the intended mould, with the centre ones to be used first. It takes the application of one piece of mat to estimate the amount of resin per square foot needed. The mats vary in weight and personal experience sometimes modifies the figure given in manufacturer's instructions. That first piece of mat probably takes at least twice the amount of resin that was used on an equivalent area of glass bandage— remember the wing joining exercise on Chapter 3. Pour out some resin and add the catalyst in the recommended proportions. Use a fresh paper or plastic cup or previously clean out the residue of gel coat from the old one. It is not recommended to mix new over old; it

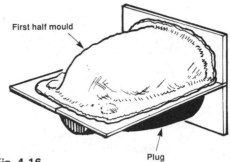

First half mould

Plug

Fig. 4.16

upsets the curing.

Apply a coat of resin over the gel coat in the area to be covered by the first piece of mat. Lay the mat in place and stipple the resin through with a flat piece of scrap wood, the brush tip, or the sponge pad. Add more resin to any areas that are still dry on top. The mat should be evenly saturated, but need not be oozing with resin. As long as the strands are sticking together, it does not matter if the surface looks like a piece of Shredded Wheat cereal.

If there is resin over, apply the next piece of mat, but if that resin is becoming stiff and rubbery, there is no point in attempting it. In this state it will not soak between the strands or bond properly. Its state will be seen as it is taken from the pot. If it goes onto the job it will pull the first piece of mat away as it sticks to the brush.

With practice, and on a small area, several pieces of mat or cloth can be laid up with one mixing of resin, particularly if the workshop is cool. So continue laying mat onto resin until the mould looks like Fig. 4.16. The flange will be a little thicker than the rest and the register cones will have been covered. There should be no mat drooping down over the edge of the ply. Very large moulds, like, for example, a whole fuselage side, can have strips of ply or softwood bonded onto them for rigidity. Leave the mould to cure to the state when it is rigid but not rock hard. Trim surplus whiskers of mat away from the

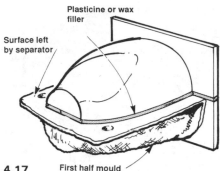

Plasticine or wax filler

Surface left by separator

Fig. 4.17 First half mould

flanges to avoid scratches on the knuckles. Insert a blunt table knife between the ply and the flange, work it around the edge and gently prise the ply out of the groove in the plug. The plug itself will remain in the first mould, as will the register cones which will have parted from the ply. Dig only these out of the flange. The mould will look like Fig. 4.17; note the exposed sawcut in the plug, which now needs to be filled and made smooth. A wipe of soft filler or Plasticene can be knifed around to meet the flange. It has to be flush with the joint edge. Check that there are no stray pieces of glass fibre on the exposed surface of the plug, then coat it and the exposed face of the glassfibre mould flange with release agent. Go through the whole lay-up procedure for this side, taking care to keep the new flange level with or slightly within the edge of the first one. Overhang here could bond the mould halves together.

When this half is cured, prise the halves apart very gently and slowly, to allow air to enter the mould. In the process, the flange may be allowed to bend slightly, it should spring back after it has parted from the plug around the edge. Ease the halves apart evenly all round. In all probability the plug will remain in one half. Ease the edges of this half mould and insert a blade in the sawcut to persuade the plug to lift out. Leave the moulds to harden, then trim up and clean out any release agent. If there are any unwanted nicks around the edge of the mould, put there in the removal of the plug, or tiny bubbles in the mould surface, apply a tiny spot of filler, made up from resin mix and plenty of filler powder. Trim it to shape or flat it off when not quite fully hardened. When all this has been done, polish the mould to restore any gloss that may have been lost during making. It is this final surface that is so important in forming a good finish on the moulding, and subsequent ones taken from the moulds for other modellers.

Drill the flanges for bolts, so that the mould can be used in one piece. The whole reason for building the mould in the manner described is to allow the moulding to be made in one piece, so that it looks just like the plug. If it is deep, it will need to be supported so that the inside is easily reached from the rear open end. Thoroughly cover the inside surface with more release agent, making sure that there are no uncoated spots, particularly on the joint line, or excesses forming puddles.

Making a moulding

Using the plug for measurement, cut mat or cloth to cover it evenly, with an extra thickness at the nose. Mix up a gel coat batch of resin, coloured if required, and paint the inside of the mould, in just the same way as described for the mould itself. It may be more difficult to reach if the cowling is very deep, so be observant over the detail if incorporated. Tilting the mould around helps to distribute the resin, but blot up excess when returned to the upright position.

Continue with the lay-up process as before. Tweezers will be useful for positioning mat or cloth, while the resin is stippled through from beneath. A stick of wood will hold the strands in place as the brush or sponge pad is lifted off.

The exposed rear edge should protrude just past the end of the mould, but resin should not be allowed to dribble down, bonding the moulding to the outside surface of the mould. Trim the rough edge of the moulding here before it becomes hard. When cure is complete (3 or 4 hours), unbolt the mould and open it as before. The open end of the moulding can be eased slightly to start the parting process. When the final moulding has been removed, clean both it and the moulds and bolt the latter together again to keep them from warping before they are needed for another job.

Finishing the moulding

Put a strip of masking tape along the edge to be trimmed to fit the model. This will hold stray strands together as they are cut away. Use a junior hacksaw blade to trim, not a power tool—the tiny fragments of glass fly about all too easily and can be breathed in. Wear a breathing pad and glasses or swimming goggles. It is better to look silly than be uncomfortable! Metal polish can be used to produce a shine on a good surface, otherwise use T-Cut, but avoid over-rubbing if there are surface details that are raised. Edges can be smoothed with wet and dry abrasive paper used wet with soap. Wash away the residue—do not blow dust about. Attach fixing brackets with more resin and bandage (tiny pieces of mat are likely to break up and finish up on the brush).

One-piece moulds

When the component is shallow and/or has clearance angles, like that in vac-forming, the mould can be made over a

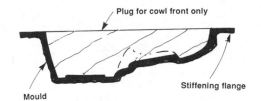

Fig. 4.18

plug mounted on a flat board, which shapes the flange. The latter merely reinforces the edge, it is not bolted to anything.

The moulding procedure is just as described for one half mould or the finished moulding as appropriate, Fig. 4.18. Most cowl fronts are suitable for this method. Wheel pants, however, even though small, need a split mould, otherwise they have to be designed like a tea cosy!

Two-piece mouldings

Some practice is advisable before making whole fuselage shells, but the technique of making the two half moulds is the same as previously described. The mouldings are made with each mould half open. The lay-up is taken up slightly past the flange edge, to be trimmed back before completely hardened, after using them to assist in freeing the shell, Fig. 4.19. The shells should come out easily, because there is such a long edge of up-stand upon which to pull. The surplus edge can be trimmed with metal shears if it has not become too hard, particularly if cloth is used, but avoid deforming the

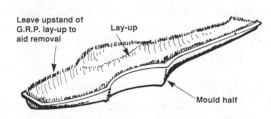

Fig. 4.19

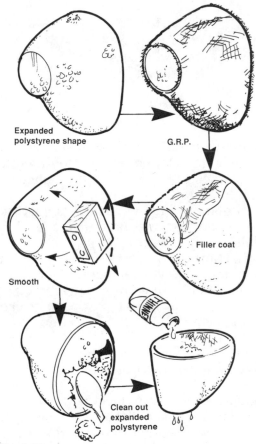

Expanded
polystyrene shape

G.R.P.

Smooth

Filler coat

Clean out
expanded
polystyrene

Fig. 4.20

edge proper. Replace the mouldings firmly back in the mould for complete warp-free curing. Joining the half shells follows the method described earlier in Chapter 2.

External lay-up

If surface detail is not required, and weight is not of prime importance (on a cowling, this is often the case) then a one-off method can be used. It involves the use of an expendable plug and a certain amount of surface finishing. Taking the example of a cowling, the method, shown in Fig. 4.20 goes as follows:

Shape a block of expanded polystyrene to a form very slightly smaller than the intended finished cowling. Smooth it to an even surface rather than a dead smooth finish. It does not need to have any clearance angles, because it will be torn apart in removing it later.

Using EPOXY resin (to avoid melting the plug just made), apply mat or cloth, the latter being preferable. No gel coat is used because the finish will be outside. When two or three layers have been laid up, go over the surface while it is still soft and press down any stray bumps and strands.

At the rubbery stage mix up an epoxy coat with plenty of filler powder. Paint this over the surface and allow it to cure to a stage when it can be sanded easily without deforming. Test a small area to see.

Using coarse wet and dry abrasive paper on a sanding block, water and soap, produce a smooth surface. Fill, with more epoxy/filler, any of those hollows which cannot be levelled without cutting into the glasscloth around them. Finish off with fine wet and dry paper.

You now have a solid cowling with a hard skin. Cut away the expanded polystyrene from the centre: an old spoon, suitably sharpened, makes a good tool for this job. There will remain a layer of expanded polystyrene adhering to the epoxy. Melt this out with petrol or paraffin and scrub it clean before adding fixing brackets or blocks with more epoxy.

Chapter 5
Integrated construction

SOARING ENTHUSIASTS will appreciate the need for strong, light wings of high aspect ratio. This chapter suggests some interesting reinforcement built into the spars and surrounding areas.

Composite spars

Spars, of necessity made shallow by the use of thin aerofoil sections, can be given better resistance to tensile stress. This can take the form of a sandwich of glass fibre strands and the hardwood of the spars, see Fig. 5.1.

Discarding chopped strand mat and woven cloth, much more strength is obtained by the use of strands of glass fibre running parallel to the length of the spars. Such strands are sold as 'Rovings' and come in bundles of varying weight, Fig. 5.2 compares them with glass cloth.

It is possible to select by hand several such groups of strands and to arrange them with short groups each side near the root end of the wing panel, graduating through several intermediate lengths to central ones carried the full span. This provides a graduated strength pattern, so that there are no weak spots, no excess thickness and no excess weight. Fig. 5.3 shows the pattern.

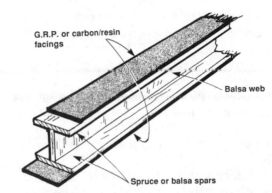

G.R.P. or carbon/resin facings

Balsa web

Spruce or balsa spars

Fig. 5.1

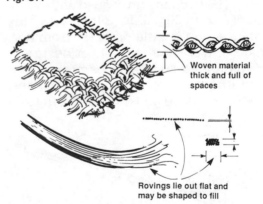

Woven material thick and full of spaces

Rovings lie out flat and may be shaped to fill

Fig. 5.2

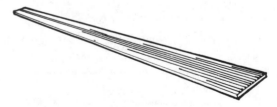

Fig. 5.3

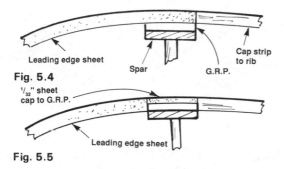

Fig. 5.4

Leading edge sheet · Spar · G.R.P. · Cap strip to rib

¹/₃₂" sheet cap to G.R.P. · Leading edge sheet

Fig. 5.5

Laminating in situ

The wood spar may be retained as a principal part of the structure, in which it may be only slightly thinner than normal, then, for example, the GRP layer can occupy say ¹⁄₃₂ in. above it, followed by the leading edge sheet, applied while the resin is wet, so bonding the three together with no external smoothing to be done. See Fig. 5.4.

Alternatively, the spar can stay where it might otherwise have been designed, ¹⁄₃₂ in. GRP added and capped with ¹⁄₃₂ in. sheet, as in Fig. 5.5. Either way, the construction is little different from normal rib, web, spar and sheet design.

Reinforced spars can be pre-assembled under more controlled conditions, however. These generally turn out to be

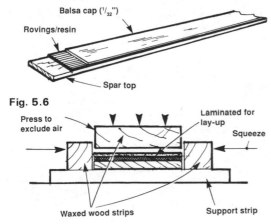

Balsa cap (¹/₃₂")
Rovings/resin
Spar top

Fig. 5.6

Press to exclude air · Laminated for lay-up · Squeeze · Waxed wood strips · Support strip

Fig. 5.7

lighter because there is no excess resin. Fig. 5.6 shows one popular method.

Take a sheet of glass or flat metal strip, (D.I.Y. shops sell 1 in. × ⅛in. light alloy strip or angle). This is the base which ensures that the spar is flat and straight. Wax the top surface to prevent the resin adhering. Prepare two straight strips of hardwood deeper than the finished spar, and wax their surfaces.

Clamp or wedge these each side of a thin spruce or balsa spar laid on the glass or alloy strip. This forms a trough as seen in Fig. 5.7. The reinforcement is laid in and covered with a strip of ¹⁄₃₂ in. balsa. A strip of hardwood no wider than the spar, and waxed underneath, is laid along the spar. Weights are placed

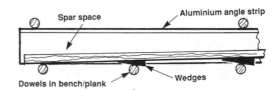

Spar space · Aluminium angle strip · Dowels in bench/plank · Wedges

Fig. 5.8

along the side strips and on the last mentioned strip. This forces excess resin out and consolidates the lay-up. Work quickly, so that the resin is still runny when the weights go on. Curing can be accelerated by the application of heat from a hair drier. Spars that are tapered in plan view can be made by this method; cut the top and bottom pieces to a taper first. If a flat alloy strip is used, it can be mounted in a board with holes drilled alongside it, so that wedges can be inserted to locate the side moulding strips of hardwood, see Fig. 5.8, which also suggests the use of alloy angle to locate one side of the spar, in place of the second wood strip. By using progressively wider wedges, or a tapering side strip, tapered spars can also be made on such a jig.

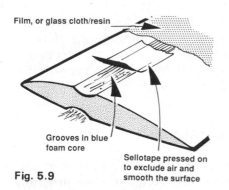

Film, or glass cloth/resin

Grooves in blue
foam core

Sellotape pressed on
to exclude air and
smooth the surface

Fig. 5.9

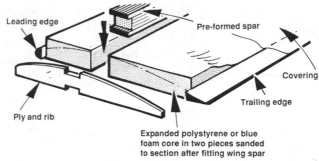

Leading edge

Pre-formed spar

Covering

Trailing edge

Ply and rib

Expanded polystyrene or blue
foam core in two pieces sanded
to section after fitting wing spar

Fig. 5.11

GRP spars in foam wings

More usually, made in blue foam, these reinforced wings can have a shallow groove cut in the top and bottom surfaces. This accepts a lay-up of GRP using rovings and epoxy. If the wing is to be film covered straight onto the foam, a strip of Sellotape is laid on the wet resin to flatten it. Then a strip of hardwood or metal is pressed onto it, to consolidate it, see Fig. 5.9. Vertical webs can be introduced by drilling the core before laying in the spar reinforcement. Balsa dowels fit the holes and become bonded in, Fig. 5.10.

If it is decided to chop through the core, as in Fig. 5.11 a composite spar can be made on the metal strip, as seen in Fig. 5.12. The elements are laid flat on their sides and excess resin scraped clear from the exposed side. Hardwood can be substituted for some of the spar

area and the depth of the spar can be varied or tapered by this method.

Box leading edges

The leading edge section of a wing can be moulded in glass cloth in place of a conventional balsa built-up framework in this area. Thin wings can benefit from this treatment, seen in Fig. 5.13. A hardwood strip is shaped to the leading edge aerofoil section back to where the spar would normally be. It is thinner than the finished section by twice the thickness of the intended moulding.

A piece of cardboard representing this thickness is temporarily spot glued over the wood and a thin aluminium strip bent to match it as seen in Fig. 5.14. Suitable for smaller spans, this needs careful shaping to fit. Alternatively a strip of covering film can be applied to

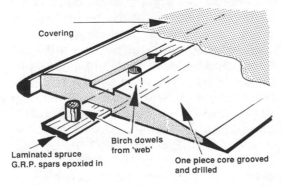

Covering

Birch dowels
from 'web'

Laminated spruce
G.R.P. spars epoxied in

One piece core grooved
and drilled

Fig. 5.10

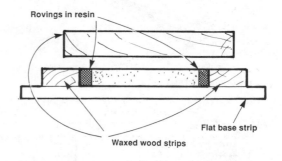

Rovings in resin

Flat base strip

Waxed wood strips

Fig. 5.12

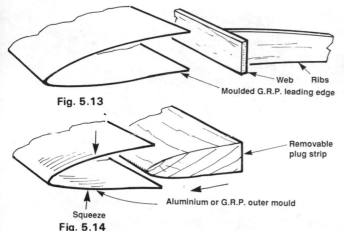

Fig. 5.13

Web Ribs
Moulded G.R.P. leading edge

Removable plug strip

Aluminium or G.R.P. outer mould

Squeeze

Fig. 5.14

the card, and given a coat of release agent. A glass fibre lay-up can be moulded over it to form a female mould. We thus have a double mould, each to be coated with release agent. One is forced over the other to stretch the resin-wetted glass cloth to the right shape and thickness and provide a smooth outer surface, for very little weight.

A less involved method is to use only the release-coated inner wood strip and lay the cloth over it, followed by a strip of polyester draughting film, suitably released, or left integral with the moulding as a smooth surface. If the film is pulled back against the wood, by taping it tem-

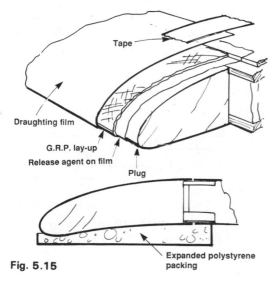

Tape

Draughting film

G.R.P. lay-up
Release agent on film

Plug

Expanded polystyrene packing

Fig. 5.15

porarily to hardwood strips, as in Fig. 5.15, thinner lamination results. If there is undercamber, however, this presents problems, but a foam strip may provide pressure underneath.

GRP reinforced L.E.

If a balsa sheet skin is to be wrapped over a foam core or used in conjunction with built-up structures, its smooth outer surface can be preserved by applying reinforcement inside. Robert Bardou from France suggests that a pre-formed strip of sheet is used, but acknowledges that unless the leading edge is very thick, the sheet will not go round it without splitting.

Ammonia is the answer. It softens the balsa temporarily, so to shape the sheet, obtain a 40in. length of plastic guttering, fix sheet styrene end caps to it with polystyrene cement and put a cupful of ammonia and water mixture (equal parts) into the trough so made. Lay the balsa sheet over the trough and wet it with a brushful of the mixture. It should bend enough to lie in the bottom of the trough to soak. Soon it will be very flexible, so transfer it to the leading edge of the wing core, or to a shaped foam strip. It will form easily over the small radius. Rubber bands hold it while it hardens. The trailing edge of the core should be reinforced with corrugated cardboard, to prevent the bands cutting in. Fig. 5.16 shows these stages.

Now tape a strip of polythene to the bench and cut a strip of light glass cloth diagonally to the weave. Lay it on the polythene and wet it thoroughly with epoxy resin. Stipple it on with a stiff brush. Roll the cloth up carefully and transfer it to the rear edge of the pre-formed balsa, now removed from the core and propped up to receive it; (Fig. 5.17). Unroll the cloth and gently slide it onto the inside face of the wood; more resin will bond it securely and further narrow strips can be added at the extreme nose area.

When partly cured, the whiskers can be trimmed off and the whole unit applied to an epoxy-coated area of the core, or bonded onto a wing spar and web system of a traditional built-up wing.

Trailing edges can be reinforced by incorporating glass cloth between upper and lower sheet skins, then sanding down to a fine edge, wing-tips can also benefit from this sandwich method. Remember, though, to avoid contact between expanded polystyrene and wet polyester resin.

Glass fibre wing skins

Foam wings can be given complete skins from lightweight glass cloth and epoxy, though the epoxy should be applied sparingly to avoid excess weight. The skins can incorporate a second layer of glass cloth in areas of stress, the resultant thickness being small enough not to require thinning the core in that area.

Balsa leading and trailing edge may be incorporated if desired, if only to get a straight edge in the soft core material while it is being handled during skinning.

The cloth is stretched over the core dry and the *thin* type epoxy applied with a wooden roller which has been covered with several layers of toilet paper. If it is rolled gently so as not to unwind the paper, this deposits a small amount of resin, yet mops up excess. A dry toilet roll can then be rolled over any areas that look too wet. The idea is to bond the fibres together, not to fill the surface, for the finish can be applied with heat shrink film if gloss is required.

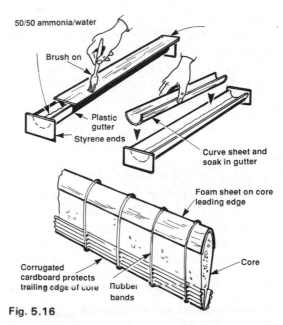

Fig. 5.16

The strongest skin results from the cloth and resin being properly consolidated on the core, there being no excess resin and certainly no air bubbles

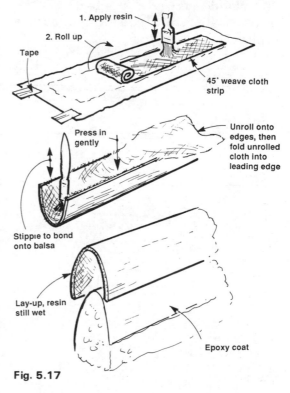

Fig. 5.17

present. The best way of ensuring this is to use a sheet of thick polythene, to form a smooth release membrane and give the surface a good finish. Smooth it tightly over the wet surface and sandwich the assembly between the blocks of waste expanded polystyrene that were cut from the core when it was first made.

Insert the whole pack into a large polythene bag, tape up the neck and exhaust the air from it. The vacuum should be maintained whilst the resin is reaching the solid state. Once it is just past the 'rubbery stage' will do. Naturally the job should be subjected to vacuum treatment while the resin is really liquid. Warmth will aid this and speed up cure.

The author uses a simple method of producing a vacuum. Many modellers have a small air compressor, used for spraying models and decorating plastic kits. Place the compressor in a ventilated wooden box so that the bag does not melt against the hot pump head. Place the pump and box in the bag with the wing or whatever. Tape the air pressure

pipe and cable together and seal them into the neck of the bag with masking tape. Switch on the pump. After a minute or so the air will have been pumped (pushed) out of the bag and a pressure of some tons applied evenly at 20 or so pounds per square inch if needed. Turn off the pump and wait. If the bag can be forced apart, switch on briefly, to restore any vacuum lost by leakage. Fig. 5.18 shows the method.

Cloth on veneer

Veneered wings can be treated in the same way, and this time the veneer helps to avoid excess epoxy resin being used. Be sure to watch for any blisters between the veneer and the cloth, which in most cases is very light and with an open weave. Traditional construction with balsa-skinned flying surfaces responds well to this all-over reinforcement, which extends to a finishing process when required.

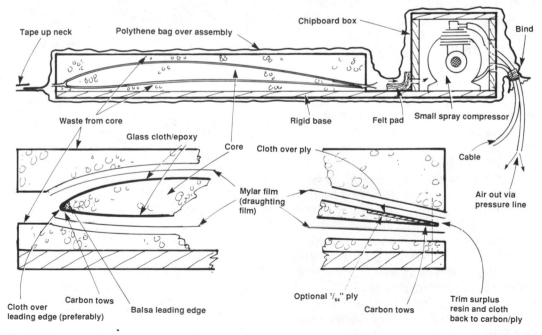

Fig. 5.18

Separate skins

A continuation of the glass skin leading edge described earlier is a rather more specialised procedure. Shown in Fig. 5.19 is one skin set up for moulding. It is the type of work that is intended for ultra high performance models. The resultant wing, made with or without webs, can be warp free and very strong for its weight. The moulds are produced by making a single cut in expanded polystyrene; the thickness of the material melted away by this hot wire cut is made up by very thin Rohacell 55 or expanded polystyrene sheet (wallpaper insulation), sandwiched between two layers of glass cloth/epoxy and polythene which is the release membrane separating them from a flexible sheet of plastic, probably thick draughting film, and the mould. A sheet of rubber provides pressure all over when the mould halves are clamped up. Alternatively the vacuum bag process may be used. This produces one skin, which itself, is double skinned. Another pair of moulds are used for the other surfaces of the wing. These are joined at leading and trailing edges, incorporating tows of glass or carbon fibre.

Carbon fibre

Much stronger than glass fibre, carbon fibre is sold by specialist GRP suppliers, usually in the form of tows, to be used instead of glass where particularly high strength is required and ideal where the limitations of the shape being built will not accommodate enough glass fibre, either in cross section or in weight. Thin strands of carbon can be placed diagonally in geodetic fashion in sheeted open frame or foam construction. Individual ribs can have a single strand placed under each cap strip, to reinforce the thin trailing edge area (Fig. 5.20).

In fact anywhere where tows are

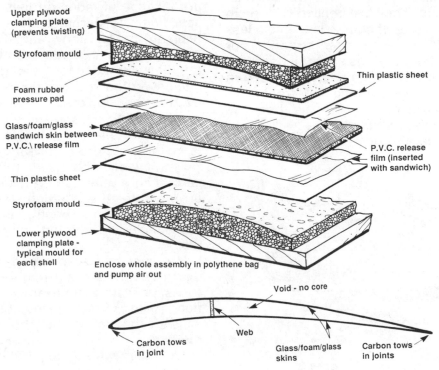

Upper plywood clamping plate (prevents twisting)

Styrofoam mould

Foam rubber pressure pad

Glass/foam/glass sandwich skin between P.V.C.\ release film

Thin plastic sheet

Styrofoam mould

Lower plywood clamping plate - typical mould for each shell

Thin plastic sheet

P.V.C. release film (inserted with sandwich)

Enclose whole assembly in polythene bag and pump air out

Void - no core

Web

Carbon tows in joint

Glass/foam/glass skins

Carbon tows in joints

Fig. 5.19

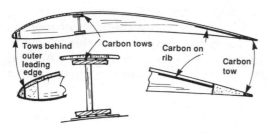

Fig. 5.20

employed, carbon fibre offers a stronger alternative, both in tensile strength and in rigidity. There is even carbon fibre cloth, though this is used only for areas where glass cloth and carbon tows alone are insufficiently strong: in thin booms, for example.

Kevlar

Kevlar and Boron are more specialised forms of reinforcement, being generally lighter and thinner than glass and carbon fibres. Available in tape form, they can be bonded after binding them around or laying them on the areas to be reinforced. They are bonded with resin as before, but of course take much less to produce the required strength. For areas where rovings are to be used, the Kevlar tape yields a source as seen in Fig. 5.21, unravelling the transverse weave, which is continuous, from the longitudinal (warp) strands.

Modellers concerned with the ultra

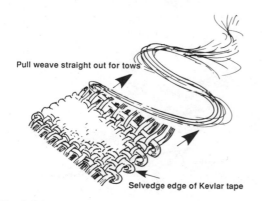

Fig. 5.21

high performance contest machines will find, by experience, where to apply these superior materials. Much useful information and inspiration can be gleaned from the free flight contest scene and from examples of man-powered and microlight aircraft. Working out the stresses in a design is a matter of individual application, so there is no scope in this handbook for specific figures. However, it is often a good policy to incorporate a tried and tested system, before trying to improve it to suit your own needs. Anything really innovative is best tested in principle by setting up a small test sample and comparing it with a more orthodox structure.

Booms and tubes

There are already sources for ready-made GRP tubes for use as fuselage booms and even wing spars. Ronytubes are a range of tapered tubes produced specifically for aeromodellers, and have been around for many years. They come in a range of diameters and lengths, originally intended for free flight gliders and power models, but also adapted for even rubber powered machines. Radio controlled gliders and some twin boom power and electric models use the larger versions from this range. Fishing rods may also be used, there being carbon fibre reinforced versions too. All are manufactured to high standards of tolerance and strength, which the modeller would have difficulty in matching.

However, we can try a few less exacting versions, starting with ballast tubes for soarers, for example. These do not have to be finished smoothly outside, so can be made by the following method.

The tubes have to be parallel bore, so

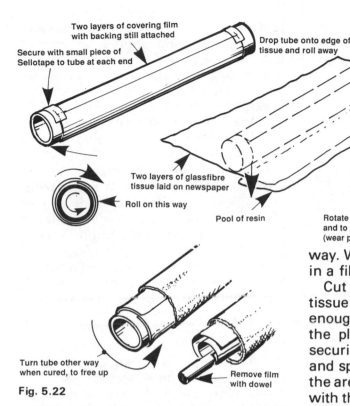

Two layers of covering film with backing still attached

Secure with small piece of Sellotape to tube at each end

Drop tube onto edge of tissue and roll away

Glassfibre lay-up

Two layers of glassfibre tissue laid on newspaper

Roll on this way

Pool of resin

Rotate in hand to consolidate and to remove excess resin (wear polythene gloves)

Turn tube other way when cured, to free up

Remove film with dowel

Fig. 5.22

the commercial versions, being tapered are excluded (unless tapered ballast is produced). Ballast should fit the tubes properly, as if it is allowed to rattle about, it could damage the structure on landing. One method of making parallel tubes for this purpose is to select a piece of metal pipe or wood dowel, of similar diameter to the ballast to be used. If the ballast is formed by casting lead in a metal tube, for example, then this tube itself will form a core plug.

The method is shown in the series of sketches in Fig. 5.22 and the most important point to watch is the use of Solarfilm or draughting film as a release membrane around the plug. When you roll up a drawing, the inside edge may spring out slightly and it is this principle that is applied in this case. Tape the film at each end to the plug. The tape must be outside the area to be treated with lay-up. Allow the film to loosen slightly then tape its outer corners in the same way. We now have a plug slightly loose in a film tube.

Cut a piece of glass cloth or finishing tissue (a very fine form of mat) large enough to go a couple of times around the plug. It must not reach the tape securing the film. Lay it on newspaper and spread a pool of resin the length of the area to be coated. With the plug held with the end of the film facing you when it is at the top, dip it into the resin and roll it onto the tissue, rotating it to pull the tissue through the resin and onto the moulding. The resin should not run under the film if it is done this way.

There will be too much resin on the job at this stage, so rotating the moulding in the same direction, lay it in the spare hand and squeeze the excess resin off. It is a messy stage, but gives the outside a better chance of fitting the holes in the ribs. Hang the moulding vertically to cure, watching out for dribbles over the tape.

When fully cured, undo the tapes and wind the plug tube or dowel in the opposite direction for the first time. This should free it. Slide it out and fish around with a thin piece of dowel, for the inner end of the film. Tape this to the dowel and go on winding. This should strip the film from the inside of the moulding. Cut the tube to length, result; one or a pair of tubes.

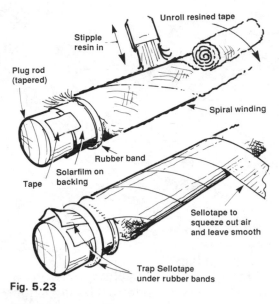

Fig. 5.23

Booms

If the boom is to be produced with a pronounced taper, a suitably tapered plug, wrapped with a release film, will do the same trick. However, the outer

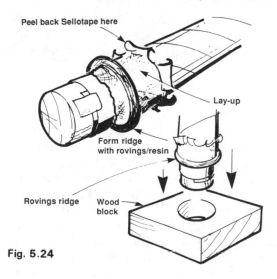

Fig. 5.24

surface needs to be better finished and the material used should be several layers of glass cloth.

It is here that the method of lay-up varies. The cloth is cut into a strip several inches wide—tape would show an edge—and wound on in a wide spiral. This results in the strands forming a geodetic reinforcement.

Secure one end with tape and wind the first layer on dry. Wet it with resin and follow with another layer of wet cloth in the same direction to tighten it and squeeze the resin through. (Fig. 5.23). Make the moulding slightly longer than required. Wind a layer of masking tape or Sellotape over the lay-up, keeping up the pressure, but holding the tape firmly where it covers the wet GRP. Practice is needed to avoid disturbing the cloth, or getting so much resin on the tape that it won't stick! When the binding is complete and the resin is cured, the outer surface should be smoother and more consistent in thickness than if it were left alone. Peel the tape back and form a reinforcing roll of strands or rovings around the thick end. When fully cured, rest this thickened end of the moulding on a short piece of thick wall tube, or on a block of wood drilled to fit over the plug. Fig. 5.24 shows the method. Free the plug by hitting the small end, rotate it to free the film and strip the tape from the outside. Dust the plug with talc and replace it for support, then sand and fill the outer surface of the moulding where it shows any unevenness. Such a boom will be heavier than a commercial version of similar size and strength.

Chapter 6
Fillets and finishing

GRP FINISHES—that is, skinning with glass cloth and resin—are durable and add reinforcement to the model without much increase in weight. Those models which lend themselves readily to the treatment are fully sheeted or veneered. The earlier stages of construction can therefore allow for this tough skin as part of the final strength, thus being a little less strong than others designed for tissue, film and paint finishes.

Apart from the application of light glass cloth as mentioned earlier, the making of fillets and the final filling can be an integral part of the finishing method now to be described. The first stage is carried out before the wing and tail panels are assembled to each other and to the fuselage.

Sand all the surfaces smooth, but do not fill small hollows. Check for fit to the fuselage and their angles in relation to each other. Join the wing halves and if in two panels, the tailplane. Use the method described in Chapter 3. The finishing of the edges of reinforcing tape are blended in, but only lightly sanded to remove bumps. The strongest job should result from the glass cloth being in close contact with the skin, not padded out on a pool of resin, Fig. 6.1.

Using light cloth of, say, ½oz (15g). per square metre, apply it to the entire surface area of each component, including the faces to be joined, like the tailplane centre. See Fig. 6.2. Use resin to join the tail components to the

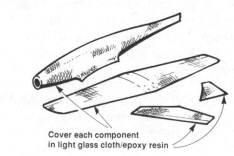

Cover each component in light glass cloth/epoxy resin

Fig. 6.1

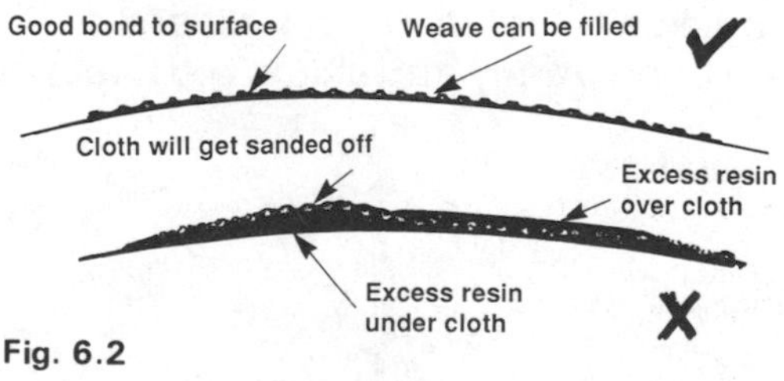

Good bond to surface   Weave can be filled ✓

Cloth will get sanded off

Excess resin over cloth

Excess resin under cloth ✗

Fig. 6.2

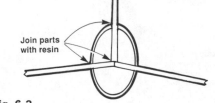

Join parts with resin

Fig. 6.3

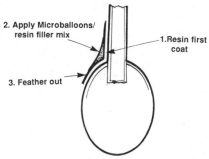

2. Apply Microballoons/resin filler mix

1. Resin first coat

3. Feather out

Fig. 6.4

fuselage; it bonds to the surface cloth perfectly and soaks into the end grain to reinforce it—Fig. 6.3.

To ensure that any gaps are filled, use a thickening filler known as micro balloons. This is composed of tiny bubbles of glass, so small that it looks like a powder. Obtainable quite cheaply from GRP suppliers, it is compatible with epoxy or polyester resin. Add it to the mixed resin in a little puddle to make a creamy paste for areas where it can be run in, or to a stiff putty suitable for spreading with a knife. We are not yet at a stage where actual fillets are to be placed. This stage is to secure and maintain alignment of the components. Filleting may disturb the alignment if it is carried out with the joint flexible and wet. Continuing to Fig. 6.4. Mix a stiff paste for filleting, but give the area where it is to be placed a lick of unthickened resin. This will ensure a good bond. Apply and shape the fillets in

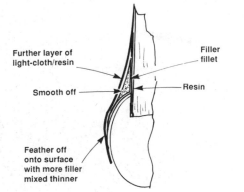

Further layer of light-cloth/resin

Smooth off

Feather off onto surface with more filler mixed thinner

Filler fillet

Resin

Fig. 6.5

the paste, using a flexible strip of plastic card or the tip of an old nylon propellor.

Allow the fillets to cure, then smooth them with wet abrasive paper, feathering them out into the resin beneath that area, applied for the purpose, not down so far that the cloth is exposed. A spot of powder paint in the resin mix will provide a tell-tale, showing how far to go.

The next stage is to give the fillets a tough surface, for although they are resin based, the micro balloons reduce the strength (so that sanding is easily done). Another piece of light glass cloth is resined on over the fillet, and when cured, given a light sanding—Fig. 6.5.

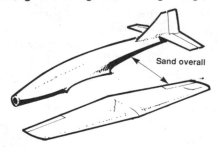

Sand overall

Fig. 6.6

Any small dents and hollows are then filled with a resin/micro balloons paste, and when cured, feathered off. At this stage, the engine bay of power models can be fuel-proofed with resin, for the final finishing stages are to follow and spilt resin would have to be tidied up.

If the control surfaces are hinged in place later, the process is easier, but if this cannot be arranged, go over all the hinges and clearance gaps with a mixture of wax and white spirit, or wax furniture polish of the block type sold in tins. This acts as a resist, preventing things getting gummed up in this area. Make up a batch of resin with enough micro balloons to give it a thin creamy consistency. Apply a thin coat to the entire model. A large model will probably need two mixes, to avoid running out of workable resin, due to the time it takes to cover the surface area effectively. The application should be even and the resultant coat enough to hide the weave of the cloth, without there being any pools of resin, which will only have to be sanded away later. Aim to have as much micro balloons as will permit this even application. If there is not enough filler, extra filling will be needed. Too much, and the application will be uneven. Fig. 6.6.

Take the model outdoors, and using medium fine abrasive paper, sand the model all over, wet. Finish with No. 600 wet if there are no hollows remaining, or spot out these with more resin/filler prior to the final rub down.

Select a paint finish that is compatible with the polyester finish just applied and apply primer and subsequent colour finishes with equal care, sanding between coats with progressively finer grades of abrasive paper. Fig. 6.7. Any

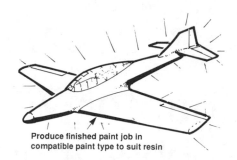

Produce finished paint job in compatible paint type to suit resin

Fig. 6.7

dummy surface detail such as panel lines and rivet heads can be put on prior to the final coats, but after the main rubbing down of the undercoats. If there are any small areas to matt down for a paint key, avoid damage to this detail by using a domestic scouring powder such as 'Vim' on a soft toothbrush or cloth. Do not dwell with water on the PVA glue dots used for simulating rivets unless they have been hardened for some days!

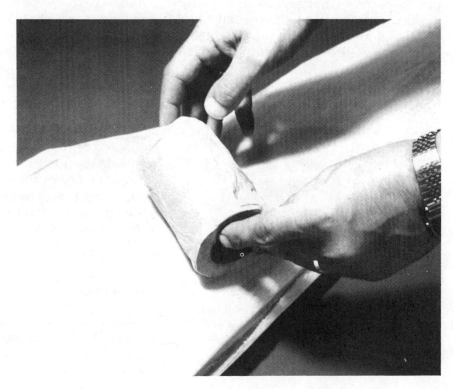

Surplus resin can be blotted up by rolling a soft toilet roll over the surface, tearing layers away as they become sodden.

Chapter 7
Rubber mouldings

ITEMS LIKE DUMMY pilots are a test of ingenuity in making a set of moulds for the production of a GRP figure or torso bust. However, there is a method which simplifies things—it is latex moulding.

In the first method to be described, the figure is cast as a thin shell in a similar style to slipware pottery, using a plaster of paris mould and a water-based, filled latex liquid. Tyres are also suitable subjects, as are small fairings which

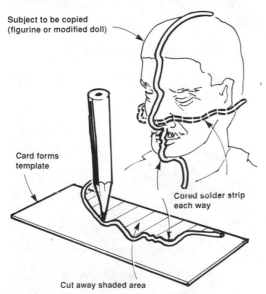

Subject to be copied
(figurine or modified doll)

Card forms
template

Cored solder strip
each way

Cut away shaded area

Fig. 7.1

have to be flexible. Starting though with a pilot figure, proceed as follows.

Drill a hole in a block of wood and insert a nail loosely into it. This is the armature upon which to model the head. Take a well-kneaded piece of Plasticine or, if you are used to working in the material, pottery type clay intended for modelling. The latter hardens to a leather-like state and can then accept carving to finalise the detail. Plasticene, on the other hand, remains softer and may be modified later. Clay can only be restored to a softer state by breaking up the discarded model and storing it in a sealed polythene bag with a little water kneaded into it. Further kneading brings it to a modelling consistency again.

Take plenty of time to get a realistic shape and features by studying photographs, or, if there is some suitable three dimensional reference, like an Action Man doll or bust of Mozart, bend a strip of cored solder around the important features, lay it on a piece of card and pencil in a line from the inner edge as in Fig. 7.1. Cut the card to make a template. Do not use the solder directly, as it will bend out of shape too easily. Repeat the process for measuring width.

Another method is to sketch the front and side portraits of the figure from a photograph enlarged to the right size, or slightly smaller, onto a piece of clear plastic. Use a chinagraph pencil. Set this up on a stand between your eye line and the model. The relationship and shape of the features can then be checked and adjusted. See Fig. 7.2. Build up in small pieces over a basic tilted egg-shaped skull. This brings more success than hacking away areas.

Care will be repaid in the finished product, for every detail will be reproduced in the moulding. Being rubber, the completed figure cannot be easily modified by carving or filling, so smooth areas have to be smoothed thoroughly, no loose bits left stuck to the face, goggles cut back to accept plastic lenses, and folds in cloth produced by actually rolling out and folding the material, rather than scratching lines. The texture of hair can be applied with brush marks of the right scale or even applied with plumbers' hemp bonded in.

A little practice in texturing will save committing the whole head to the moulding stage in the wrong state. Make up a series of blobs of clay or Plasticine on a small board, texture and finish them, take a plaster cast and use that to familiarise yourself with the rest of the process as well. It is suggested that the first moulding is of the head alone, for the torso can be separate, then the finished components joined to give the head a realistic sideways glance, a pleasant change from the frozen, sometimes petrified forward stare!

The mould

When satisfied with the clay stage, find a small cardboard box or piece of plastic cup. Leaving the head on its nail for the

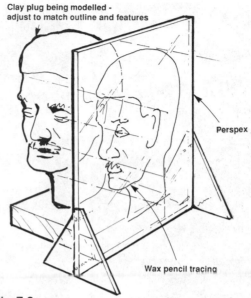

Clay plug being modelled - adjust to match outline and features

Perspex

Wax pencil tracing

Fig. 7.2

moment, as in Fig. 7.3, put a few tablespoonsful of water in a plastic cup, then sprinkle Plaster of Paris in, working it to a creamy consistency. It should be thin, not like double whipped cream. Flick this onto the rear surface of the model (plug) until it is covered, then set the head face up in the box. Pour the remaining plaster mix around it, without splashing the face. Stop when it is covered half way up (around the ears).

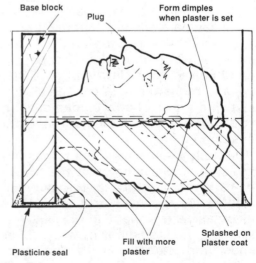

Base block

Plug

Form dimples when plaster is set

Plasticine seal

Fill with more plaster

Splashed on plaster coat

Fig. 7.3

Left, clay head ready for moulding. Right, two unfinished figures straight from the mould.

Tap very gently to dispel bubbles and allow it to set for an hour or so. Drill two register hollows with a penknife—a countersink also will do the job.

Paint a little washing-up liquid onto the plaster around the head, going right up to the model. This is the release agent for the mould joint. Make up more plaster and flick onto the exposed model, top up with more poured on. Large moulds can be reinforced with medical bandage in the plaster. A torso mould can be made like that in Fig. 7.4. Only when the plaster is hard and strong, several hours later, prise the mould halves apart, leaving the plastic cup or cardboard box aside. The clay or Plasticine will probably be damaged in extracting it from the mould, but it will have done its job.

Carefully clean away any remaining pieces from the hollows of the mould and carve an aperture for the mould to be filled via the neck. Put the mould halves aside overnight to dry out. Re-assemble the mould halves with rubber bands and stand it with the neck opening uppermost (Fig. 7.5).

The latex, which is type AL360W, comes from Dunlop Semtex Ltd., who will advise you of the nearest supply agent. It comes in a minimum 5 litre can, but is not expensive and can be used for attaching veneer to foam wing cores as well.

Shake well, allow to stand for 15 minutes to disperse bubbles then open and pour some into the mould. Tap the mould to clear air bubbles. The latex will slowly be absorbed, so top up gradually. After anything from 4 to 10 minutes, depending on how thick the moulding is to be, pour the still liquid latex back into the can and replace the lid. Shake the can to seal it again. Leave the mould draining neck down for the next 10 minutes, then allow the moulding to dry out. It should be touch dry in 2 or 3 hours at room temperature. It can be hurried in the oven for about 15–20 minutes at 60 degrees C.

The latex will have shrunk slightly at the exposed edge. Carefully separate the mould, encouraging the moulding to stay in the half it prefers. Shake a little talc over, and inside it, and gently ease the moulding away from the mould join line. As it comes out it will be very flexible, so once freed, it can be returned to the mould to harden a little. Some hours later it will be quite easy to handle and can have any flash removed with a small grinding stone on a miniature drill, or with an emery board. More latex or contact adhesive is used to join the head to the torso when it has been made. Artists' acrylic colours take well on the cleaned surface of the latex. Their flexibility preserves adhesion.

Latex tyres can be moulded in the same way, but keep turning the mould over to keep the latex thickness even and to avoid bare patches on the side where the filler hole is sited. (Fig. 7.6).

Points to remember

The flexibility of the finished moulding permits undercuts to be incorporated, so it is possible to mould shapes which would not normally come cleanly out in GRP.

The dry plaster absorbs water from the latex, so what is left is the filled latex only. A damp mould results in a thinner moulding for a given time of standing, prior to draining. If the residue is swilled around in the mould, it washes the accumulation of latex away, leaving a bald or thin patch. Large bubbles leave holes in a thin moulding. Inspect the inside and spot them out with more drops of latex before putting away to harden.

Some more bulbous tyre sections defeat the one-piece moulding method. Try again with the half moulds open, then join the tyre half-shells with contact adhesive or cyano. Reinforce inside with more latex or silicone rubber bath sealant, or Bostik rubber caulking. The tyres can be painted with black tyre paint (motor accessory shops).

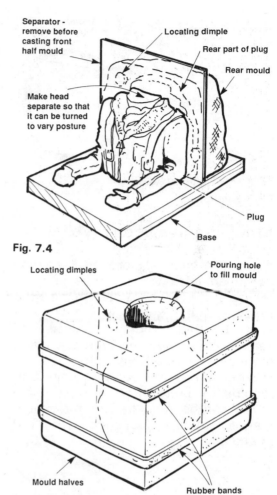

Fig. 7.4

Fig. 7.5

The moulding need not stop at the tyre, whole hubs have been modelled using small nuts and other detail. The final moulding is then reinforced on the inside of the hub with GRP and bushed with brass tube, see Fig. 7.7.

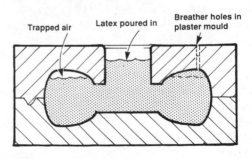

Fig. 7.6

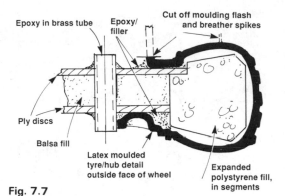

Epoxy in brass tube
Epoxy/filler
Cut off moulding flash and breather spikes
Ply discs
Balsa fill
Latex moulded tyre/hub detail outside face of wheel
Expanded polystyrene fill, in segments

Fig. 7.7

Moulding in silicone rubber

Silicone rubber is more resilient than the filled latex and it cures at room temperature when exposed to the air. A ready source of supply is the hardware shop. It is sold in plunger tubes as bath sealant, in a range of colours and black; the logical choice here.

While it may be moulded from plaster moulds, a better and more durable mould can be made in GRP in a similar manner to that described for GRP mouldings.

However good the quality of the moulding, the finished result will also depend on your skill at painting the items.

Chapter 8
Repairs with and to GRP

WHEN IT COMES to the 'crunch', few materials are so adaptable to reinforce a damaged aircraft as glass and resin. On its own, epoxy of the 'five minute' variety has, for many years, been used to effect field repairs to balsa and other traditional structures. Few modellers seem to have taken the precaution of including glass cloth in their field kit.

This chapter illustrates not only those 'quickie' repairs but shows how to deal with the more involved repair jobs needing workshop facilities for accurate and safe restoration.

On the spot

Is the damaged area wet, is it fuel soaked? These two major factors determine whether the epoxy will bond properly. On a typically rotten damp flying day, the model will probably need to be dried off in the car with the heater going full blast. The epoxy will run into the grain readily if the latter is warm, otherwise it may sit on the surface in a shiny blob, add weight and little strength.

If the model is a power job, drain the tank to avoid even more oil getting onto the area to be repaired. Strip away soggy iron-on film, that may be hiding more damage, trapping fuel and generally getting in the way. If there is oil present, the epoxy will not bond properly, so rub the area with a de-greasing agent like lighter fuel or carbon-tetrachloride. In Britain a substitute for carbon-tet called 'Thawpit' has been used for many years, both for cleaning clothes and on the flying field, Cellulose thinners not only softens the film adhesive, but cleans the wood; it is also useful for cleaning paint-brushes that have been used for resin (before fully cured, that is).

Any soft and soggy wood needs to be cut away, which will expose fresh, clean wood (hopefully) or at least make the cleaning easier. New wood, bonded in with epoxy and a few strands of glass rovings stripped from a piece of cloth, should restore the strength of, say, a cracked leading edge strip or stringer.

Where to stop

Minor dents and scuffs, secondary spars and small sheet splits can be tackled on the field, but repairs to foam wings, main spars, load bearing longerons and around the engine department should be dealt with at home, when the urgency to be airborne again is left behind. To attempt a major repair on the field, particularly on a power model or weighty scale model, could result in a write-off, damage to other models, or worse; injury to people. Besides, with the proper workshop facilities, the repair can be done once and for all, with the minimum weight penalty. It can be done tidily, without having to trim back and re-do a field patch.

Small dents

If minor dents and splits are tackled on the field, bearing in mind the foregoing, consider using a car body repair filler paste, which after being rubbed well into the balsa grain may be scraped level and sanded smooth. A piece of masking tape will protect it from the weather until it can be smoothed further and painted or covered with an iron-on film patch.

Remember, however, that most such fillers are polyester based, so may not bond well to epoxy repairs. Cyano applied initially to make a firm joint, however, will be satisfactory. It is also excellent for bonding stray strands of glass fibre disturbed in a surface failure of either polyester or epoxy bonded GRP.

Major repairs

At home, check to see if the part is repairable. It may be safer to re-build, particularly in the case of foam wings damaged further inboard than, say, ⅛ from the tip, on any panel. It is easy to underestimate the load on a wing in aerobatic flight or on tow and in any event a repair may take longer than a rebuild, certainly if the damage is a crush-inflicted one. Resolve then to repair only lightly stressed foam wings and in the area mentioned.

Leading edge damage is dealt with by cutting through the entire damaged area, foam core and veneer together until a sound part of the core is revealed. Trim back with a sharp blade to produce an even surface, so that the joint is thin.

Cut a block of expanded polystyrene of similar density to the damaged piece. Glue it in with epoxy or PVA. Micro balloons in the epoxy will help to fill the gaps and not impair the strength (which is far higher than the EP itself).

Shape it to match the adjacent areas in Fig. 8.1. Scarf in a new piece of balsa leading edge to match, but with a junior hacksaw, slit each side behind it and insert a piece of epoxy coated glass cloth, using a piece of thin metal or a postcard to get the loose strands in tidily (Fig. 8.2). Fit the new leading edge strip and fold the top and bottom edges of the cloth back onto the new core piece; fit the leading edge strip over it

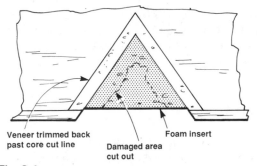

Veneer trimmed back past core cut line

Foam insert

Damaged area cut out

Fig. 8.1

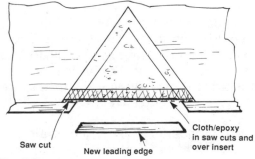

Saw cut

New leading edge

Cloth/epoxy in saw cuts and over insert

Fig. 8.2

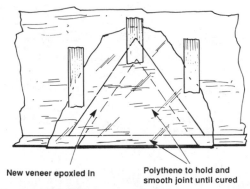

New veneer epoxied in

Polythene to hold and smooth joint until cured

Fig. 8.3

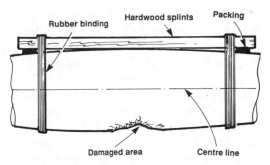

Rubber binding   Hardwood splints   Packing

Damaged area   Centre line

Fig. 8.5

while it is still wet. If there is time apply new veneer to fit, otherwise hold the cloth down with a piece of polythene, tightly taped in place. See Fig. 8.3. The glass reinforcement should improve the joint between the patch and the wing. The veneer can be butt joined with cyano, but do not be lavish with this as it melts the polystyrene!

If the veneer is slightly split and creased, but the core resists denting with finger pressure, then glass cloth can be epoxied over to restore its strength. Apply with enough micro balloons in the epoxy to partly fill the weave and blend out each side to avoid a sharp transition between bare veneer

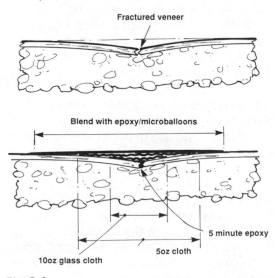

Fractured veneer

Blend with epoxy/microballoons

5 minute epoxy

10oz glass cloth

5oz cloth

Fig. 8.4

and strong patch. This helps to avoid a weak point. Fig. 8.4 illustrates this detail.

Repairs to grp components

Glass fibre fuselages may have surface damage caused by excessive flexing or hard contact with something else. The gel coat crazes and if self-coloured appears lighter in shade. Cyano glue will generally soak into the tiny cracks and restore the strength. Do not sand the surface first, the dust prevents penetration of the thin cyano. The thicker types of cyano should not be used, for the same reason. Cyano can also be used to penetrate a crack in the joint between fuselage half shells.

If such a fuselage can be twisted, this method may not be enough, so the method of fuselage joining described in Chapter 4 should be followed. Cyano will hold things true while it is being done.

Where the gel coat is broken and pieces flake off, it is a sure sign that the main glass laminations are weakened. If resin were to be applied at this stage, it would not fully penetrate the tiny spaces between the separated or broken glass fibres. Drip cyano onto the broken fibres, which will secure them prior to going over with resin and micro balloons to restore the finish. Be sure to use the same type of resin.

If the fuselage or boom is bent, one side will be caved in. To repair this type of damage, locate the fuselage in a jig made from strip wood, or cut a piece of hardwood and use it as a splint. This works for straight taper fuselages and booms. If the sides are of dual curvature near the damage, insert packing wedges as in Fig. 8.5, to keep the centre aligned. Apply cyano to the damaged glass strands, after pushing the dent out from inside with a pad of foam rubber on a stick. Needless to say, the task is tricky and if there are pushrods, these should be removed first, (they are probably broken or bent too).

If the dent cannot be reached from inside, drill a hole in the dented area and insert a hooked piece of wire, held in place by a second splint and wedge, as in Fig. 8.6. Apply the cyano and let it harden fully before doing any cutting or filing of the glass fibre. The cyano stops bits flying about and prevents the edges going furry. It ensures that those fibres are firm before the glass cloth and resin patch is applied in the area shaped to receive it. See Fig. 8.7.

To blend the repair into the rest of the fuselage, sand the adjacent gel coat down a little, apply cyano to seal stray strands that may then be exposed, then

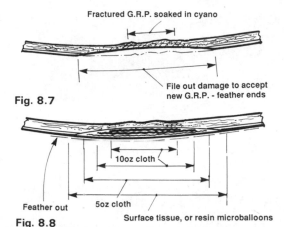

Fractured G.R.P. soaked in cyano

File out damage to accept new G.R.P. - feather ends

Fig. 8.7

10oz cloth

Feather out   5oz cloth

Fig. 8.8   Surface tissue, or resin microballoons

wind on a strip of light glass cloth with resin and micro balloons. Follow with a binding of polythene strip to give it a smooth surface—Fig. 8.8. The glass cloth will conform to the fuselage shape better if it is cut with the weave at 45 degrees. Ensure that it is fully wetted with resin (not too much micro balloons). A final finish can be applied by fairing in with car body filler—elastic type is best. Rub down wet with abrasive paper, finishing with fine grades.

Complete breaks

Remove all linkages, including snakes. Trim back all loose pieces with knife and metal shears. Do not use a power tool—it throws broken glass about. Clean the area with cellulose thinners and sand lightly inside and out.

Measure the fuselage from the plan to determine the length to be replaced. Mark this distance in the building board. Insert a piece of paper in the larger part of the fuselage and mark the size of the internal section of fuselage to be replaced. Allow an inch or so each side of the break, and a small overlap to make such a tube. This method, as seen in Fig. 8.9, works for almost any cross section.

10 oz. glasscloth cut at 45 degrees to match the paper pattern is then resin

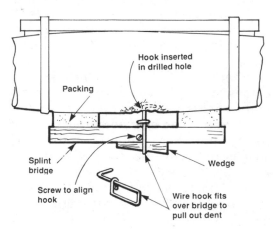

Hook inserted in drilled hole

Packing

Splint bridge

Screw to align hook

Wedge

Wire hook fits over bridge to pull out dent

Fig. 8.6

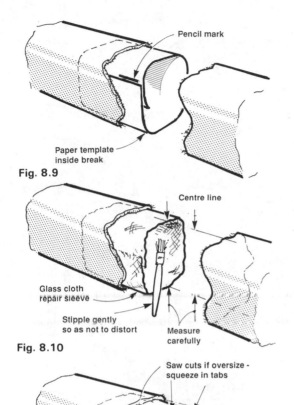

Fig. 8.9

Labels in Fig. 8.9: Pencil mark; Paper template inside break

Fig. 8.10

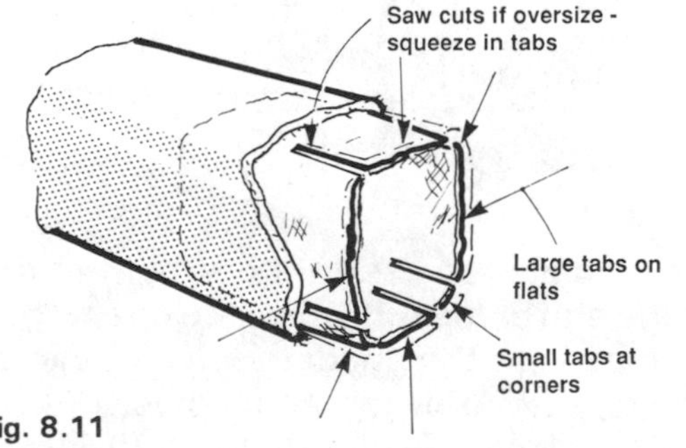

Labels in Fig. 8.10: Centre line; Glass cloth repair sleeve; Stipple gently so as not to distort; Measure carefully

Fig. 8.11

Labels in Fig. 8.11: Saw cuts if oversize - squeeze in tabs; Large tabs on flats; Small tabs at corners

If it is too tight to insert, slit the spigot lengthwise with a junior hacksaw and squeeze it in to fit. This is best tested before the spigot is cured really hard, but not until it is firm enough not to become detached from the larger half. Fig. 8.11 shows the slitting of the spigot.

When a fit is effected, apply resin to the rear fuselage inside and wedge the halves together. Use splints, wood blocks or Plasticine lumps on the board to align it with the reference marks put there earlier. Fig. 8.12. When fully cured, remove the fuselage from the board, and with a coarse half round file, make a depression on the outside to accept an external patch. Apply cyano to loose strands exposed in the process, then resin in place a narrow strip of 5oz. glass cloth in the centre of the depression, all round the repair joint. Follow immediately with a wide piece of coated and inserted in the larger end of the repair, shaping it by increasing the overlap until it is about the right size to fit the smaller end. This is something to be done by eye, so as not to get resin on the other half, or to distort the patch sleeve, which will become a locating spigot when cured, Fig. 8.10.

It may be better to use cloth cut square to the weave if the length of the spigot is such that the cloth is difficult to keep firm in the early stages of application. When cured, the spigot is inserted in the smaller end of the fuselage. If it is a slack fit, apply a layer or two of light skinning cloth and allow to cure again.

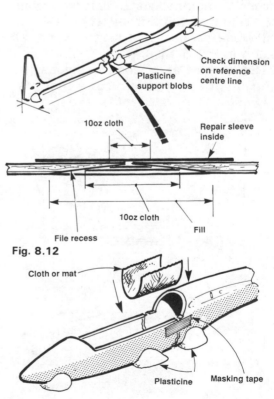

Labels in Fig. 8.12: Check dimension on reference centre line; Plasticine support blobs; 10oz cloth; Repair sleeve inside; 10oz cloth; File recess; Fill

Fig. 8.12

Labels in Fig. 8.13: Cloth or mat; Plasticine; Masking tape

Fig. 8.13

5oz. cloth to spread the load and thickness to blend in. Allow to cure then fill and finish as before.

Where a break occurs near an opening, such as at the end of a hatch or canopy, and may be easily reached, a piece of 10oz. cloth or thin chopped strand mat may be used to repair the inside surface. (Fig. 8.13). Support the fuselage on blobs of Plasticine and follow the method described earlier, including the application of cyano.

Mending broken tubes

A complete break in a tubular GRP boom tube can be repaired by the following methods: 1. Insert a new piece of Ronytube to fit—one might find it easier to fit a whole new tube as it has to be bought anyway, but perhaps a suitable piece remains on a discarded model. 2. Wind a tube from ¹⁄₆₄ in. (.4mm) plywood, to use as a splice spigot, as seen in Fig. 8.14.

Some pod and boom fuselages are made with internal structure that pre-

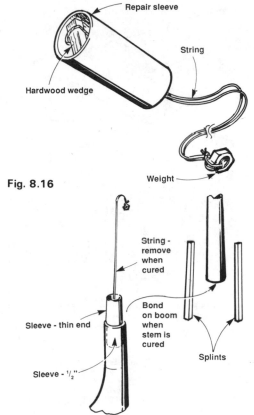

Fig. 8.16

Fig. 8.17

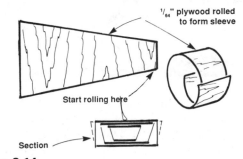

Fig. 8.14

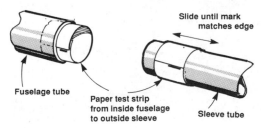

Fig. 8.15

vents clear access to the whole of the large end of the tube from the opening in the pod. If the model is NOT one of these, then proceed as follows.

Cut a slice of tube that will fit inside both halves. This is easily done by rolling a piece of paper into a tube and inserting it into the broken end as in Fig. 8.15. Mark where it overlaps and use this to check *over* the sleeve tube. The thickness of the paper gives clearance for the resin.

The slice of repair tube should have a length of about three times its diameter. Wedge a piece of spruce into the thick end and loop string over it and through the tube (Fig. 8.16). Feed it down the fuselage from the front. A weight may be used to get it down there. Pull the tube through until it reaches the joint. If it fits, push the tube back into the pod

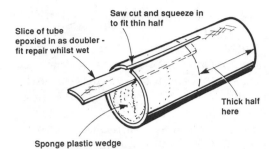

Fig. 8.18

Slice of tube epoxied in as doubler - fit repair whilst wet

Saw cut and squeeze in to fit thin half

Thick half here

Sponge plastic wedge

and tape the string to the fuselage boom at the repair point. At this stage, resin coat the outside of the repair tube.

Hold the fuselage nose up and pull the tube into place (Fig. 8.17). Wipe excess resin from the protruding half and check that it sticks out straight. Leave to cure, remove the string and wood wedge, then re-coat with resin and fit the tail end of the boom. Splints keep the boom straight until cured. Now just fill the joint line.

If the tube cannot be inserted from the front, saw it lengthwise and squeeze it into place in the resined boom ends. Splint as before. The split tube is not so strong, so double the sawcut line with a strip cut from a tube offcut resined in place as in Fig. 8.18. The tube can be made longer; say four diameters.

Appendix 1

Hints and tips

RATHER THAN WRITE similar ideas into each chapter, these little reminders can be easily found here, for some apply to subjects in several chapters. They might be missed when reading about other subjects or applications, and mentioning them only once means that we have been able to get more into the book than space would otherwise allow.

Check the temperature of the workshop before mixing resins. They set/cure faster when it is hot.

Use a hair drier or similar gentle heat source to speed up cure. Resin hardens more quickly in the mixing pot than when spread out thinly—do not mix more than can be handled in one go. Never under-estimate the time it takes to stipple resin thoroughly into the glass mat or cloth—otherwise the brush will stick to the cloth and lift it.

Use a thixotropic additive to resins used on vertical surfaces—useful on deep mouldings.

Add micro balloons as a filler to the resin to give it body and to save weight when filling—it sands easily.

Do not add it where great strength is needed—it is better to compress the glass strands than to make up with resin. Remember rovings give superior strength, weight for weight, compared with cloth.

For more strength in confined spaces like sharp trailing edges, carbon fibre tows can be spread out thinly—stronger than glass tows.

Mat absorbs much more resin—best used only at the nose area. Trim edges with metal shears when rigid but before rock hard. Do not use power sanders—broken glass is injurious to health—wear a breathing mask when working dry GRP, or trimming cloth edges.

Polyester resin and cyano both melt expanded polystyrene. Epoxy resin does not adhere properly to polyester mouldings; polyester resins do not adhere properly to epoxy mouldings; cyano adheres to both. Both adhere to cyano.

A soft balsa plug may be deformed by heavy vac forming pressure. Fill and smooth the plug surface, but do not polish it to a mirror finish—the air has to escape in vac forming. A plug for GRP mould making may be highly finished, but remember to use release agent.

PVA glue can be used as a release agent when thinned with 60 per cent water. Do not apply it to moulds that are in several parts, or it will glue them together.

Provided joints between plug parts are sealed with wax, PVA can be coated over for release.

Wax plugs need no clearance, as they can be melted out—but of course can only be used once.

Rubber moulds also need no clearance, since they stretch to remove the moulding. They are too soft to be used without a GRP or plaster outside casing—make sure this comes off first or you are back to square one.

Items moulded in rubber can be collapsed to allow withdrawal from a rigid mould.

Latex mouldings depend on absorption or evaporation of the water in the liquid to leave a precipitation of latex in the mould—Plaster of Paris moulds should be dry before use.

Silicon rubber mouldings can be made in GRP, plaster, Plasticine, wax or metal moulds, but air has to reach the material.

Resins, once mixed with their catalyst or hardener, cannot be prevented from curing, but cooling slows the process.

Once cured, they cannot revert to a liquid.

Any resin left on tools, brushes or in a mixing pot should be scraped off while rubbery in texture, then the items cleaned with cellulose thinners and dried.

Foam plastic pads can be used instead of a paint-brush when it needs to be expendable. A paint brush should be stiff: soft bristles do not stipple the resin in properly.

Bend a small brush at right angles near the bristle end, join it to a long wood dowel to reach inside fuselage seams.

Polythene stretched over an outside application of GRP, so that there are no wrinkles, reduces the amount of finishing work—it leaves a smooth surface.

A nylon scouring pad helps to take the resin off the hands, when used with pan cleaning powder or washing-up liquid.

When it's time to paint, use a compatible finish, including undercoat, to the final surface of the model, whether the latter is made or filled with polyester or epoxy resin.

Keep a record of the type of moulding resins and finishes used, so that when a repair or re-paint is needed, a suitable match and bond will result. Pass this information on to whoever owns the model when you have finished with it.

Appendix 2

Useful addresses

Fibre Glass Aircraft: 1 Charlton Gardens, 37 Charlton Road, Wantage, OX12 8EL. Suppliers of Rovlok non woven uni-directional reinforcement fibre sheet.

Sheffield Insulation—Branches throughout the country. Suppliers of 'Blue' Foam.

Fibre Reinforced Products: 9 Minehead Grove, St. Helens, Merseyside, WA9 4BP. Tel. 0744 816337. Contact: Graham Bingley. Suppliers of G.R.P. Materials: Kevlar, Boron, Carbon-fibre, polyesters and epoxies.

Dunlop Semtex Ltd., Industrial Products Division, Chester Road, Birmingham B35 7AL. Tel. 021 373 8101.

Alec Tiranti Ltd., 21 Goodge Place, London or 70 High Street, Theale, Berks. Suppliers of clay and plaster, release agents and moulding and glass fibre materials.

Strand Glass, Wollaston, Northants.

K & B Manufacturing Incorporated, PO Box 809, 12152 Woodruff Avenue, Downey, California 90241. Suppliers of fibreglass cloth.

Mid West Products Company, 400 South Indiana Street, PO Box 564, Hobart, Indiana 46342. Suppliers of fibreglass cloth.

Fig Manufacturing Company, 401–7 South Front Street, Montezuma, I.A. 50171. Suppliers of fibreglass cloth.

Aerospace Composite Products, PO Box 16621, Dept. M. Irvine, California 92714.

Composite Aircraft Engine and Supply, PO Box 866, Lapeer, Michigan 48446.

Subscribe now...

here's 4 good reasons why!

Within each issue these four informative magazines provide the expertise, advice and inspiration you need to keep abreast of developments in the exciting field of model aviation.

With regular new designs to build, practical features that take the mysteries out of construction, reports and detailed descriptions of the techniques and ideas of the pioneering aircraft modellers all over the world – they represent four of the very best reasons for taking out a subscription.

You need never miss a single issue or a single minute of aeromodelling pleasure again!

	U.K.	Europe	Middle East	Far East	Rest of World
Aeromodeller *Published monthly*	£23.40	£28.20	£28.40	£30.20	£28.70
Radio Modeller *Published monthly*	£15.60	£21.20	£21.40	£23.60	£21.80
RCM&E *Published monthly*	£15.60	£21.60	£21.80	£24.00	£22.20
Radio Control Scale Aircraft *Published quarterly*	£9.00	£11.10	£11.20	£12.00	£11.30

Your remittance with delivery details should be sent to:

The Subscriptions Manager (CG/16)
Argus Specialist Publications
  1 Golden Square LONDON W1R 3AB.